DON'T WORRY, BE HAPPY!

Finding Happiness at Work, at Home and at Play

Samuel A. Malone

The Liffey Press

Published by
The Liffey Press
Ashbrook House, 10 Main Street
Raheny, Dublin 5, Ireland
www.theliffeypress.com

A catalogue record of this book is
available from the British Library.

ISBN 978-1-905785-62-9

Printed in the United Kingdom by Athenaeum Press.

Don't Worry, Be Happy!

About the Author

Samuel Malone has many years' experience as a training consultant, training manager and lecturer. He has an M.Ed (in training and development) from the University of Sheffield and is a qualified Chartered Management Accountant. He is the author of thirteen books including *The Ten Skills of Highly Successful People* and *People Skills for Managers* (The Liffey Press). He lives in Dublin.

CONTENTS

PREFACE

The purpose of this book is to explore the subject of happiness at work, at home and at play in a practical, clear and understandable way. The book is guided by personal experience and research rather than hearsay and anecdote. It will act as an antidote to the current climate of recession and gloom and doom. People can improve their level of happiness by becoming more aware of the things that make them happy and by undertaking the activities at the end of each chapter.

The purpose of life is to be happy. Surveys on happiness consistently show that people throughout the world desire the same things in order to be happy including a descent standard of living, a good family and social life, a nice neighbourhood in which to live, good health and a satisfying job. Health, beauty, money and power are highly valued because we expect them to make us happy. Generally, they do, but not always. The "Hedonic Treadmill" means that you need to keep running to have your happiness stand still. We gradually adapt to ever higher standards of living and take things for granted so that we are no happier than before.

Comparing ourselves with those who are better off may engender feelings of envy and resentment rather than happiness. You will feel happier if you compare yourself with those who are less well off than you are. Happy people are more likely to be extroverts than introverts. People find the greatest sense of happiness during flow experiences. Happiness occurs in moments so that you should savour the good moment when it happens.

It would be naïve to think that money is irrelevant to happiness. It provides you with a descent standard of living and gives many benefits like independence, security of mind and freedom from financial worries. Celebrity and fame may bring misery to some rather than happiness. In contrast, people who live a simple frugal lifestyle are often happy. Happiness rises as people are lifted out of extreme poverty and are able to afford the basic necessities of life.

Good relationships are an important source of happiness. Relationships are nurtured by love and displays of affection. They are undermined by contempt and constant criticism. Married people report more happiness than those who are unmarried, living together, divorced or separated. Self-confidence will help you make friends easily. Trust is a vital ingredient of friendship and once broken it is almost impossible to renew the friendship.

People with a calling enjoy their work and are very happy because they find their job intrinsically rewarding. There are many ways to be happier at work including doing work that you enjoy and being comfortable with the organisation and people you work with. People need an appropriate work–life balance to be happy.

The authoritative parenting style is a high discipline and high participative style and achieves the most successful outcomes in the rearing of children. Intuitively you would think that children make parents happy but the research is mixed and often seems to suggest otherwise. Though challenging and burdensome, many people find parenthood a meaningful role providing a sense of purpose in life. However, even with the best of parenting skills some children turn out bad and become a source of torment and worry to their parents.

Optimism is how you view situations while self-esteem is how you evaluate yourself. Both make an important contribution to personal happiness. People with high self-efficacy are able to perform successfully within their area of expertise and live happy and successful lives.

Put a smile on your face to induce feelings of well-being and happiness. Laughter is contagious and helps people form and maintain friendships. Humour helps people to be happier in their personal lives and more productive in the workplace.

Looking after yourself is an important part of happiness. Sleep, exercise, diet, relaxation and spirituality will help you keep a sound mind in a sound body. Lifelong learners are happier and more successful in life. Better educated people live longer because they make more informed decisions about their careers, health and lifestyle. An ethical life is a happy life. People are happiest when they are contributing towards the welfare of others.

Happiness means having meaningful goals and enjoying the process of achieving them. Reaching the goal will only bring short-term happiness. The happiness is in the journey striving after goals. Life is all about setting new challenges as soon as existing goals are achieved. Happiness doesn't happen by chance but must be planned for and made happen through a happiness plan and a programme of activities.

Managing your stress is an essential part of being happy. Problems in life can be solved if they are tackled in a systematic and positive way with persistence and determination. If the uplifts/hassles ratio is positive it will help you cope with the little stresses of life successfully. Extreme stress can result in burnout and depression. Depressed people are very unhappy.

The positive emotions for happiness include courage, gratitude, compassion, forgiveness, humility, generosity and hope. If you want to be happy and successful in your personal life and career managing time effectively is essential. Happy people are never bored as they always have something to do. Happy people organise their lives so that they spend less time working and more time playing.

So, enjoy the book ... and don't worry, be happy!

Samuel A. Malone
September 2009

I

WHAT WE KNOW ABOUT HAPPINESS

- ❖ *Where are people happy?*
- ❖ *What is the function of happiness?*
- ❖ *What is happiness?*
- ❖ *How does age affect happiness?*
- ❖ *What is adaptation?*

INTRODUCTION

Happiness is derived from the Icelandic word "happ", meaning luck or chance. However, happiness is not just something that happens by chance or is our birthright but has to be worked on and planned for. Philosophers of antiquity and modern psychologists agree that the purpose of life is to be happy. Surveys on happiness consistently show that people throughout the world desire the same things in order to be happy, including a descent standard of living, a good family and social life, a nice neighbourhood in which to live, good health and a satisfying job.

> *"Happiness is the meaning and the purpose of life, the whole aim and end of human existence"* – **Aristotle**

Health, beauty, money and power are highly valued because we expect them to make us happy. Often they do, but not always. Beyond a certain point more money does not guarantee happiness. People do get happier as they get older, however the transition from work to retirement can be difficult unless it is planned.

FUNCTION OF HAPPINESS

We strive to feel contented and avoid pain. This helps us to survive and stay alive. A child instinctively withdraws its hand from something that is very hot because it does not want the pain of a burn. It is programmed to avoid pain and stay alive. Similarly, the fight or flight response tells us when we should face up to danger or run. We thus tend to be drawn to those things which make us happy and tend to avoid things that make us unhappy. Basically, we are motivated to seek pleasure and avoid pain. What we perceive as pleasurable attracts us and what we perceive as painful repels us. Some of us learn to deny ourselves today for future gratification as evidenced by our desire to save and plan for our future. Our ability to delay gratification is thus a good predictor of future happiness.

> *"Pleasure is an important component of the quality of life, but by itself does not bring happiness. Pleasure helps to maintain order, but by itself cannot create a new order in consciousness."* – Mihaly Csikszentmihalyi

Pleasure, however, is ephemeral and gives us only a temporary lift. Happiness is a long-term inner feeling of contentment or peace of mind. Contentment is about accepting things as they are. As a well-known saying goes, *change what you can, accept what you cannot and have the wisdom to know the difference.* Moderation in all things and self-discipline are keys to happiness. Thus people who lack self-discipline and indulge in drugs, alcohol, food and sex to excess will become very unhappy and often die prematurely. In modern society, with trends such as instant messaging and speed dating, most people have difficulty postponing gratification. Thus people no longer have the discipline of not eating between meals and moderating their alcohol intake.

Distinction between Pleasure and Enjoyment

Psychologists make a distinction between pleasure and enjoyment. Freud formulated the Pleasure Principle, which stated that our basic and strongest motivation in life is the drive to experience pleasure and to avoid pain. Pleasure is the good feeling that comes from satisfying needs such as hunger, thirst, sex and bodily comfort. Enjoyment, on the other hand, refers to the good feelings people experience when they do something that stretches them such as fulfilling some larger purpose, sporting performance, completing a worthwhile task, a good deed or a stimulating conversation. Enjoyment, rather than pleasure, leads to personal growth and long-term happiness. Nobel laureate Daniel Kahneman found that people's top four favourite parts of the day feature sex, socialising after work, dinner and relaxing. The bottom four involved commuting, work, child care and housework.

Obviously, happiness can vary from person to person and is of an ephemeral nature, coming and going and often lasting for moments only. For one person, it may be the ability to feel satisfied with life. For another, it may be the opportunity to have fun and freedom. For others, it's the absence of anxiety, stress, illness or money worries. Certainly it means making wise choices in your life and being able to read situations accurately. Happiness is greatest when we combine frequent good experiences with a few intense ones. Good experiences include having an interesting job, a loving spouse, a supportive family and an absorbing hobby. Intense experiences may include a romantic getaway, the birth of a new baby, a job promotion, or getting first place in an important professional examination.

> *"Most people are about as happy as they make up their minds to be."* – Abraham Lincoln

Serving a purpose greater than oneself and one that is in harmony with your values and beliefs is a great source of satisfaction. People who set out to put right the wrongs and injustices in the world often achieve great contentment and happiness. Mother Teresa was moved by the great poverty she saw on the streets of Calcutta and dedicated her life to doing something about it. However, most people pursue pleasure rather than enjoyment. They prefer to watch television rather than read an interesting book. We know that television is unlikely to add to our happiness whereas a good book will create flow and enhance our understanding of life.

"The great and glorious masterpiece of man is to live with purpose." – Michel de Montaigne

---

THE STUDY OF HAPPINESS

The study of happiness has a long history. Aristippus, a Greek philosopher from the fourth century B.C., taught that the goal of life is to experience the maximum amount of pleasure, and that happiness is the totality of one's pleasurable moments. In Christian thought most pleasure was seen as sinful and a distraction from the worthwhile pursuit of virtue. Happiness was not of this world but something to be aspired to in the next. Theologians believed happiness was achieved by being near to God. Strangely, we often have to experience pain, misery and discomfort before we can really appreciate happiness.

The Greek philosopher Epicurus taught that all a person needs in order to be happy are the basic necessities of life: food, water, shelter and warmth – plus friendship, freedom and thought. He advocated a simple life, arguing that although each of us has the capacity to be happy, many people make themselves unhappy by poisoning their lives with needless desires, anxieties and fear. Another Greek philosopher, Aristotle, pointed out that people pursue money, power, material possessions, beauty or fame because they believe these will bring happiness. However, he identified happiness not with the pursuit of wealth but with virtuous activity and in a life of intellectual contemplation. He identified four cardinal virtues for happiness: courage, temperance, practical wisdom and justice. He concluded that happiness was the ultimate goal in life. The British utilitarian philosopher Jeremy Bentham identified happiness with pleasure and subjective satisfaction. He believed people had the right to pursue their own happiness as they saw fit and that society should strive for the greatest happiness for the greatest number. This idea has underpinned efforts by governments to raise gross national product (GNP) and individual wealth in order to make their citizens happier. Increased wealth seemed to be a good way to increase happiness. However, GNP is not an all-encompassing measure of happiness. Its primary purpose is to measure economic activity. It doesn't measure other things that contribute to our happiness. In fact, developing reliable measures of happiness is still a work in progress. Bentham's godson, John Stuart Mill, claimed intellectual pleasures were superior to physical ones and believed that the achievement of happiness was the purpose of life. However, he also believed that those who achieve happiness have their minds fixed on some other object such as the well-being of others or some art or pursuit.

"The purpose of life is not to be happy. It is to be useful, to be honourable, to be compassionate, to have it make some difference that you have lived and lived well." – **Ralph Waldo Emerson**

THREE FORMS OF HAPPINESS

Martin Seligman, one of the pioneers of positive psychology, has identified three forms of happiness:

1. **The pleasant life.** This concerns positive emotions about the past, present and future. Positive emotions about the past include contentment, fulfilment, pride, satisfaction and serenity. Positive emotions about the present include sensory delights derived from immediate pleasures such as absorption in work, music or other people. Positive emotions

about the future include optimism, confidence, trust, hope and faith. The pleasant life is about getting pleasure out of the basic things in life such as friendships, the natural environment and bodily needs. This is what most people think of when considering whether or not they are happy moment to moment. Some people take shortcuts to achieve the pleasant life by taking drugs, drinking alcohol to excess, overindulging in food or engaging in mindless entertainment.

2. **The engaged life.** The engaged life is one filled with absorption, interest, immersion and flow. This comes through deep engagement in work, family life or other activities that you enjoy. When we do some activity that absorbs us we often get into a state of flow where there is no consciousness of time. Finding flow is about discovering your unique strengths such as kindness, integrity and wisdom and employing them creatively to enhance your life. There seems to be no genetic constraints on the engaged life. All you have to do is identify your signature strengths and use them in worthwhile pursuits. For example, a person with the signature strength of creativity could be encouraged to take up pottery, photography, writing, sculpture or painting. A person with the signature strength of curiosity could be encouraged to undertake research on some topic that interests them. Since most of us spend so much time working, having an interesting and satisfying job can make a significant contribution to your overall level of happiness.

3. **The meaningful life.** This comes from dedication to an institution or a cause greater than oneself such as family, politics, a charity or a religion and is unlikely to be influenced by genes. It might include becoming an expert in something or passing on your knowledge and skill by mentoring others. We become truly fulfilled and enhance our self-esteem if we employ our unique strengths to make life easier for others. One large-scale study compared the psy-

chology of elderly volunteers with non-volunteers. It found that retired people over 65 who volunteered rated significantly higher on life satisfaction and will to live, and had fewer symptoms of depression.

HAPPINESS AND SUCCESS

The relationship between happiness and success is reciprocal, that is, generally successful people are happy. Successful people are happy provided they work at the right activities which they enjoy while being dedicated to a purpose. They also like to feel that their work will be meaningful and will benefit others. They know that happiness is achieved while enjoying the journey. In fact, there is often an anti-climax when the goal has been achieved – a feeling of a void in one's life. Thus there is a need to discover new goals in substitution of the previous ones to keep you interested, committed, occupied and challenged.

"Success is not the key to happiness. Happiness is the key to success. If you love what you are doing, you will be successful." – **Albert Schweitzer**

Happiness, according to William James, the noted nineteenth century philosopher/psychologist, is reflected in the ratio of one's accomplishments to one's aspirations. We can thus increase our happiness by adding to our list of accomplishments or lowering our expectations. Positive psychologists have even devised a formula for happiness. It is: $H = S+C+V$. Where H is your level of happiness, S is your set point, C is the conditions of your life, and V is the voluntary activities you partake in. In other words, your happiness consists of how naturally happy you are, plus whatever is going on in your life affecting your happiness, plus the voluntary work that you do. Voluntary work has been found to add greatly to peoples' level of happiness.

HAPPINESS AND AGE

The relationship between happiness and age is counterintuitive. The common stereotype is that older people are grumpy and so one expects people to be unhappy as they get older. However, surveys show the opposite is true' Getting older is a happy experience for most people and older people feel little envy for the younger generation as they've been there and done that. The midlife crisis is often feared but scientists have found that people get more confident and agreeable as they grow older as happiness follows a U-shaped curve – it peaks when we are 20 and 70 and slumps in the middle years leaving us most miserable between 40 and 50. In fact, instead of a crisis, many middle aged people are at the peak of their success in terms of their power and influence, abilities, job and finances.

Midlife is often a time for reflection and reassessment. You acknowledge what you have achieved and look forward to what remains to be done. You are no longer burdened with fierce ambition and high expectations. Only one person in the company can become chief executive and you begin to realise that it's not going to be you. You're unlikely to win the Nobel Prize too. We were told as children that we could achieve anything we set our minds to, but now we realise that for the vast majority this is not so. It may also be a time for "wake-up" calls. A serious accident, loss of job or illness in midlife often leads to a major reassessment about the priorities in life. In addition, many people will have experienced friends or close relatives who have become seriously ill, become incapacitated or died in middle age after a prolonged battle with cancer, and this can trigger off a new appreciation for life. Furthermore, middle aged adults are more likely to experience the trauma and stress of the death of their own parents.

> *"Age puzzles me. I thought it was a quiet time. My seventies were interesting and fairly serene, but my eighties are passionate. I grow more intense as I age."*
> **– Florida Scott-Maxwell**

Embrace and Enjoy Old Age

The U-shaped curve suggests that instead of fearing old age we should embrace and enjoy it. Encouragingly, by the time you're 70, if you are still physically fit, then on average you are as happy and mentally healthy as a 20-year-old. Many people who are in good shape in their seventies still consider themselves to be middle aged. Many middle-aged people typically report feeling about 10 years younger than they are. Feeling younger than one's age is associated with greater health and happiness. Studies show that the incidence of major depression decreases with age. One study found that the 10 years after retirement seems to be the happiest and least stressful time in most people's lives.

While older people may not remember names as well as younger people, new research in 2008 by the Stanford Centre on Longevity into cognitive functioning shows they have an uncanny ability to focus on the positive side of life. It seems that ageing helps us ignore the negative aspects of life and shift our focus toward the positive. Older people experience positive emotions for longer periods of time than younger people, and they are quicker at getting rid of negative emotions. They realise that life is too short for holding grudges and resentments. The philosopher Heidegger said the only way to really feel alive is to be constantly aware that you're going to die. If you think you have an infinite amount of time you won't learn to appreciate the here and now. Older people restructure their memories by thinking about the good times rather than the bad.

The Challenge of Retirement

Most people look forward to retirement, however the transition from work can be difficult and sometimes traumatic, particularly if the process is haphazard rather than planned. You will need to be thinking about and planning your retirement for five years before you retire. It might even be a good idea to take night classes to update skills or develop new ones which will help keep you employed at any age. Your plan should take into account that you are likely to be living on a reduced income. Research confirms that financial security predicts better health and happiness in retirement. Planning for the social and psychological aspects of retirement is just as important as financial planning. Retirement should be viewed as a psychological journey, involving the need to restructure time, adopt a new role identity, redefine social relationships, and find new goals and purpose in life.

Those who retire voluntarily are happier than those who are forced to retire. Those who retire early to pursue interests close to their hearts report greater satisfaction with retirement than any other group. Obviously, these people view retirement as a new opportunity and a new lease of life rather than as an escape from the stress and drudgery of their jobs. Those who continue to work full-time after their retirement are less satisfied than those who work part-time. Retirees who are married report greater happiness than those who are not. This applies to both men and women and is consistent across cultures. Married women are generally happier in retirement than unmarried women. Divorced and separated women experience the greatest financial instability in retirement and are more likely to report low levels of happiness. Couples who had a good friendly relationship and easy relaxed communication before they retired are likely to be happy after retirement.

"A lot of our friends complain about their retirement. We tell them to get a life." – Larry Laser

---

ADAPTATION

Happiness surveys show, not surprisingly, that people in poor countries are not as happy as ones in more developed nations. Similarly, people in totalitarian and communist regimes are not as happy as those in democracies. It seems people put considerable value on their personal freedom and control over their own lives. Wealthy people are only marginally happier than those who only have enough for their needs. Obviously, we need sufficient money to live and lead a comfortable lifestyle, but beyond a certain point more money does not guarantee further happiness.

Psychologists have named this phenomenon the "Hedonic Treadmill". The pursuit of happiness is like a person on a treadmill who has to keep working just to stay in the same place. The things we expect to bring lasting happiness rarely do. We just get used to the new comforts and take them for granted. We pursue greater happiness by setting new goals, and pursuing new relationships. This process is known as adaptation or habituation. Losing 10 pounds in weight, getting promoted or winning a major prize will give a peak in happiness but then we settle back into being just as happy as we were before.

Yesterday's luxuries become today's necessities and tomorrow's relics. It seems more is never enough and thus increases in living standards haven't made us necessarily happier. We just come to expect a higher standard of living so that we are relatively no better off. People may think that a bigger house or new car will make them happier, but if it means a bigger mortgage or increased debt this may in fact put them under financial pressure and make them less happy in the long term. On the other hand, an argument with one's spouse or failing an exam makes us unhappy but seldom for more than a few days.

"A house may be large or small, and as long as the surrounding houses are equally small, it satisfies all social demands for a dwelling. But, if a palace rises beside the little house, the little house shrinks into a hut." – **Karl Marx**

Instant Gratification

Marketing people know that the average person is inherently greedy. Our wants are much greater than our needs and are often out of control. Our needs are simple. We need food, drink, shelter and companionship. Our wants for second homes, better cars, designer shoes, breast implants, patio furniture, mobile phones with all sorts of gimmicks and modern high definition televisions are insatiable and are exploited by consumerism, marketing and materialism. Marketing promotes the act of shopping as a way of finding happiness. We have become a throw-away society getting rid of clothes that have been barely worn and replacing them with more fashionable items. In fact, our pursuit of more and more has made us unhappy, unhealthy, exhausted and often in debt. Marketing also exploits our need for status in providing branded goods priced at premium prices to meet this need. We have become a culture of instant gratification. Delayed gratification should be fostered from an early age by encouraging people to save.

According to a survey in 2007 by Scottish Widows, having fun now is the biggest priority for most people in the UK. It takes priority ahead of saving for a child's future, getting on the property ladder, looking good and studying for an extra qualification. The survey also found that instant gratification gives the most pleasure such as holidays, spending money and shopping rather than spending on capital goods. The greatest fear people had was not having enough money to provide for old age, being incapacitated and unable to work and look after themselves. Nevertheless, people are not saving regularly for their future despite having these fears.

"Affluenza" is the term that has been coined to describe this phenomenon. This condition is characterised by anxiety, overload, debt, distress, greed and profligacy. People buy things they don't really need and often get into debt to do so. People should avoid debt, as living beyond your means causes endless worry, stress and unhappiness. Living high on credit cards gets you used to a standard of living you can't afford and will eventually get you into financial distress. "Affluenza" was probably one of the major reasons behind the great recession of recent years.

"If you want happiness for a year, inherit a fortune; if you want happiness for a lifetime; help someone else." – **Chinese proverb**

Keeping Things in Perspective

We all assume that more income, comfort, possessions and goods will make us happier. We don't realise that adaptation will come into play and raise our expectations to a higher level. Getting wealthier and acquiring more possessions will not make us happier as we continually try to keep up with our peers. Consequently, most people spend a disproportionate amount of their lives working to make money, and sacrifice family life, friendships, health and the attainment of personal goals; not realising that these have a more lasting effect on happiness.

Life is uncertain and you can't anticipate the problems and adverse circumstances that tomorrow may bring. If you think you have no control over what may happen you can control the way you respond and the way you perceive situations. New circumstances will present new challenges. Adversity may alter your life radically and affect relationships but it may also present opportunities. Adaptation means that we have an in-built mechanism to get used to even the most difficult situations and rise to meet the most adverse and dire circumstances. It means that many people who lose their businesses and homes through bankruptcy are able to bounce back and start all over again.

> *"The mind of every man, in a longer or shorter time, returns to its natural and usual state of tranquillity. In prosperity, after a certain time, it falls back to that state; in adversity, after a certain time, it rises up to it."* – **Adam Smith**

INFLUENCING YOUR HAPPINESS

So humans are very resilient and adaptable, and even in difficult circumstances can return to reasonably happy lives. This is helped if we have a high genetic disposition to be happy. We can be up to 50 per cent predisposed to happiness because of the genes we inherit. We can influence up to 40 per cent of our happiness by taking control of our daily thoughts and actions. The remaining 10 per cent is related to our life circumstances, such as where we live, our income, our experiences, marital status and our appearance. This means that you can do a lot yourself to influence your level of happiness.

Happiness is like our cholesterol level – partially genetically determined but also influenced by the things we do such as diet, lifestyle and exercise. This is why some people are naturally positive while others are naturally dour. Though genes play a part in our disposition there is much scope to influence our level of happiness by practising the art of happiness, getting involved in activities that make us happy and adopting a positive outlook. Remember, what you focus your attention on grows. So it pays to focus on the positive and on the things that you enjoy doing. We can think ourselves into a new way of acting and act ourselves into a new way of thinking. Psychologists maintain that simply choosing to be and acting happy can be habit forming and life changing.

Happiness in the form of self-actualisation is the highest of the hierarchy of goals according to the famous psychologist, Maslow. At the basic levels we need food, water, shelter and sufficient money for a comfortable lifestyle. At the next level we need to feel secure from external danger and need peace of mind in the form of a permanent job and a pension when we retire. We also need to feel connected with others and thus relationships are important. The average person desires respect and status. Ultimately, we want to become truly happy by being self-actualised and achieving our purpose in life and becoming what we are capable of becoming, although Maslow felt very few people achieved this state. Carl Rogers, one of the founders of the humanistic approach to psychology, expressed this as living in a way which truly expresses your individuality. We need to use our full capacities by being engaged and challenged by meaningful activities. Without a purpose, making money becomes meaningless. Thus rich pop stars and business people sometimes get disillusioned with their lives and become altruistic by giving away millions to charitable causes. They begin to realise there is more to life than just making money.

There is greater satisfaction and happiness to be gained by being generous and helping others.

"People tend to overestimate the amount of satisfaction they will get from material things and underestimate the satisfaction they derive from human connection." – John Helliwell

---

SUMMARY

The function of happiness is to feel contented and avoid pain. This helps us to stay healthy and alive. Pleasure is ephemeral. Moderation and self-discipline is the key to happiness.

Happiness has been defined as a state of joy and freedom from want and distress. Generally, successful people are happy and happy people are successful. Successful people do work that interests them while being dedicated to a purpose. They know that most of the happiness is achieved while enjoying the journey.

The relationship between happiness and age is counterintuitive. The most common stereotype is that older people are grumpy and so one expects people to be unhappy as they get older. However, surveys show the opposite to be the case. This is the paradox of ageing. Contrary to popular belief, getting older is a happy experience for most people and older people feel little envy for the younger generation. Many people look forward to retirement. However, the transition from work to retirement can be difficult and sometimes traumatic, particularly if the process is haphazard and unplanned. You will need to be thinking about planning your retirement for the five years before you retire.

Wealthy people are only marginally happier than those who have enough for their needs. The "Hedonic Treadmill" means that you need to keep running to have your happiness stand still. We gradually adapt to newer higher standards of living and take things for granted so that we are no happier than before. Happiness seems elusive as we are always striving after something better.

Five Activities to Improve Your Happiness

1) Begin and end each day with positive thoughts. Reflect on the things in life to be grateful for. Identify the things that you feel will make you happy such as more time for yourself, more time with your family, more foreign holidays, more fun, and so on. Think about the happiest day in your life and recall this event over and over again.

2) Today and every day drink and eat moderately. Moderation in all things and self discipline is the key to happiness.

3) Bad things happen to good people. Be prepared to take the rough with the smooth. Mentally prepare yourself for the ups and downs in life. Plan as to how you will deal with the inevitable things that will happen in your life so that you are not caught off-guard.

4) Work hard and be prepared to make sacrifices for the things that you desire. Save a little and spend a little should be your motto. If all your wishes were met without effort you would be bored. Get rid of that credit card! Living high on credit cards gets you used to a standard of living you can't afford and will eventually get you into financial distress and a great deal of unhappiness.

5) If you are five years from retirement age start the process of planning for retirement now. If you want to continue working after retirement think about the skills you will need and take up courses now to fill those needs.

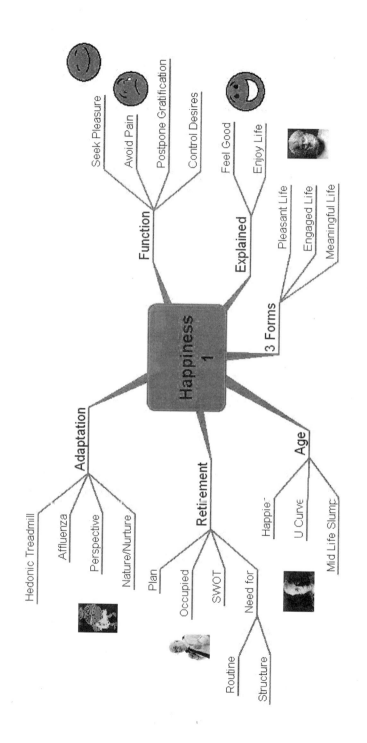

Happiness 1

Function
- Seek Pleasure
- Avoid Pain
- Postpone Gratification
- Control Desires

Explained
- Feel Good
- Enjoy Life

3 Forms
- Pleasant Life
- Engaged Life
- Meaningful Life

Adaptation
- Hedonic Treadmill
- Affluenza
- Perspective
- Nature/Nurture

Retirement
- Plan
- Occupied
- SWOT
- Need for
  - Routine
  - Structure

Age
- Happier
- U Curve
- Mid Life Slump

2

THINKING YOURSELF HAPPY

- ❖ *How can you programme your brain to be happy?*
- ❖ *What do you need to do to avoid being miserable?*
- ❖ *How does personality affect happiness?*
- ❖ *How can you think yourself happy?*

INTRODUCTION

The human brain is plastic and has an insatiable appetite for learning. Change your brain by changing your ideas and your experience. In surveys the majority of people say they are happy. Happy children usually grow up to be happy adults. Personality type may be a predictor of the level of happiness that you will achieve. Comparing ourselves with those who are better off may engender feelings of envy and resentment rather than happiness. Happy people are more likely to be extroverts rather than introverts. You are what you think about all day long. To become a happy person, think happy thoughts and get rid of negative ones.

THE BRAIN AND HAPPINESS

Your brain is flexible and loves to learn. Change your brain by changing your ideas and your experiences. The brains of London taxi drivers are thicker in the regions that specialise in visual-spatial memories. The brains of pianists are thicker in the region that specialise in fine motor movements. Negative or positive attitudes begin in infancy where the connections in our brain are laid down and evolve in response to experience. This means that experience strengthens existing neurons and creates new ones. An experiment showed that the neurons in the hippocampus of rats in an enriched environment grew by 15 per cent. These findings highlight the fact that you can change your brain by undertaking new and challenging activities and life-long learning.

Severe traumatic experiences can damage your brain. Research indicates that 25 per cent of those who experience post traumatic stress disorder (PTSD) suffer long-term effects. In addition, physical changes occur in the brain as a result of PTSD. The hippocampus, which is a structure that lies deep in the brain and is responsible for storing new memories, is smaller in PTSD victims. Repeated episodes of depression create marked physical changes in the brain that make a person even more vulnerable to depression in the future. In extreme cases of trauma or depression, the hippocampus can shrink by 10-20 per cent, impairing the brain's ability to remember positive experiences. So negative and positive experiences can produce enduring changes in the physical structure of your brain. They can affect your physical and mental health in the short term and long term.

"We've learned over the past few decades that there are strategies you can use that can actually change the brain, change behaviour and then mood and understanding follow." - Alan Kazdin

---

Our brain has been primed by evolution to naturally emphasise negative experiences. We remember failures and negative events more vividly than successes. We dwell on what went badly rather than what went well. The feelings associated with a negative job event such as a demotion, a reprimand or a cut in pay linger on and tend to play on our minds and drag us down emotionally. Negative experiences were the greatest threat to our survival in the past so our ancestors passed on these genes to us. Sadness warns us to be cautious and save energy, while disgust urges us to avoid contaminated food. Anger helps us to defend ourselves from threats. In contrast, positive experiences are usually received through standard memory systems and thus need to be held in conscious awareness 10 to 20 seconds for them to be registered in long-term memory. The elation associated with a pay increase or a promotion is often short-lived. It seems that when life goes smoothly we take things for granted unless we consciously want to remember a particularly important event.

Focus on the Positive

You can counteract this natural tendency to emphasise negative experiences by consciously focusing on the positive. Pay attention to the good things in the world and the positive things that happen to you. Set yourself the daily goal of taking notice of the beauty of nature in the world and the kindness that is extended to you each day. You can do this by making positive memories as vivid as possible and bringing them to mind frequently over an extended period of time. Savouring the positive has many psychological benefits such as increased resilience, improved moods and a feeling of optimism. These will act as a bulwark against depression and counteract trauma in your life.

Recent discoveries in neuroscience show that the ageing brain is more flexible and adaptable than previously thought. It seems that the brain's left and right hemispheres become better integrated during middle age, giving us greater creativity. Age also seems to dampen some negative emotions. In brain imaging studies, older adults show less evidence of fear, anger and hatred than younger adults. Psychological studies confirm that impression, indicating that older adults are less impulsive and less likely to dwell on their negative feeling. Common sense tells us that older brains have learned more than younger ones. The brain of a 50-year-old looks like a dense forest of interlocking branches, reflecting deeper knowledge, more experience and better judgement. That's why age is such an advantage in eminent fields like law, medicine, architecture, science and management.

> **"Happiness consists in activity. It is a running stream, not a stagnant pool."** – **John Mason Good**

The Weather Can Affect Your Mood

Apparently a lack of sunshine can affect your brain. Seasonal affective disorder (SAD) is a condition in which your moods change with the seasons. Sufferers tend to feel depressed in winter and feel better in spring. More people commit suicide in December, when the days are shortest and the nights are longest, than in any other month of the year. Lack of sufficient sunlight creates an imbalance of certain chemicals in the brain. Exposure to bright light for two to four hours a day can relieve depression in some people. So do yourself a favour and get out in the daylight for a few hours each day. The exercise and fresh air will also stimulate your brain, improve your concentration and help you sleep better at night. Phototherapy, involving the exposure to strong artificial light tubes that mimic daylight, is also said to be effective. SAD affects more women than men and is less common among children, adolescents and the elderly.

Even the weather can affect your level of happiness. Light rain seems to have little effect but extreme weather conditions is detrimental to your level of happiness. So don't think you're unusual if you feel down in the dumps when it's pouring rain outside. The novelty of snow brings happiness to children while it poses problems for adults commuting to work. Despite what you think, moving from a wet climate like Ireland or England to a sunny one like Spain or Italy will only keep you happy for a short time as you will eventually adapt to it and take it for granted.

HAPPY PEOPLE VS UNHAPPY PEOPLE

In surveys, the majority of people say they are happy while a minority claim they are very happy. Happiness tends to remain stable over a lifetime. Happy children usually become happy adults. Happy people are grateful for what they have such as fond memories and loving relationships and do not constantly make unfavourable comparisons with others. A person's level of happiness is determined by comparisons we make with standards. These standards may be based on social comparisons or on personal expectations. If people exceed these standards, they will be happy; but if they fall short, they will be unhappy.

Young girls in particular are often unhappy with their weight and appearance and want to be as thin as some of their role models like Posh Spice or Britney Spears. Happy people tend to have an exaggerated view of their talents and skills in relation to what other people think. They also tend to be happy with their looks and weight. People who are satisfied with their financial position are more likely to be happy as financial worries are a great source of unhappiness.

> *"It isn't what you have, or who you are, or where you are, or what you are doing that makes you happy or unhappy. It is what you think about."* **– Dale Carnegie**

Happy people think positive thoughts, replay happy memories in their minds and exude happiness to those around them. You can't have positive and negative thoughts at the same time so obviously it's better to think positively. Compared with the depressed, happy people are less self-focused, less hostile, and less prone to disease. Happy people are aware that they can create happy experiences in their lives and prevent many negative experiences from happening. One way of doing this is to avoid excessive drinking. Those who drink in moderation are happier than those who don't. Another way of doing this is to avoid negative people. These people are emotional vampires who will suck you dry and fill you with negativity. Obviously things happen over which you have no control. Disappointments are a part of life; you've got to go with the flow and take them in your stride. In the meantime, enjoy life as worry serves no purpose. Worry is like blood pressure: you need a certain amount to live, but too much can kill you.

"Worry gives a small thing a big shadow."– **Swedish Proverb**

Most people like to be admired and valued so happy people focus on the good points in people rather than the worst. They thus attract and retain friendships. They relate well to others and talk to people they care about. They tend to have strong ties and commitments to others. They are optimistic about their futures and begin each morning enthusiastic about the day ahead. They are in control of their lives and are not afraid to move out of their comfort zones to experiment and do challenging things. They believe that the success they achieve is due to their own efforts and that failure is caused by others and won't last. They are open to a variety of experiences and are lifelong learners.

PERSONALITY AND HAPPINESS

Personality type may be a predictor of the level of happiness that you will achieve. Studies show that extroverts are happier, even when on their own, and are happier than Introverts whether they live alone or with others, or work in social or non-social jobs. Extroverts are more outwardly-focused and involved with people and usually have a wider circle of friends. They are more likely to be assertive, self-confident and possess superior social skills. They consequently engage in rewarding social activities. They experience more affection and enjoy more social support. People enjoy being around extroverts because they are more fun and pleasant to be with, accepting of others and themselves and more confident.

Introverts are more likely to be shy and passive. Introverts tend to be more internally-focused, paying more attention to

internal thoughts. They are often socially unskilled and avoid social events that others enjoy. Introverts are not consigned to
being unhappy but need to develop a more outgoing personality
in order to make friends and relate successfully to other people.
On the other hand, some introverts are happy because they have
learned to enjoy their own company.

> **"Of all the means that wisdom provides to help one's
> entire life in happiness, the greatest by far is the pos-
> session of friendship."** – Epicurus

HOW TO BE MISERABLE

There are certain things you can do to guarantee misery:

- Brood continually on your weaknesses and problems and
  remind yourself of your inadequacies and shortcomings.

- Habitually tell lies and become totally untrustworthy in the
  eyes of others. Unreliable people finish up with few friends.

- Procrastinate and do nothing to solve problems and rectify
  situations. If you fail to address little issues they have a
  habit of becoming major problems with the passage of
  time. You ignore health warnings and only take the appropriate remedial action when it's too late.

- Humiliate people around you by continually finding fault
  with their actions. Offer casual insults during conversation
  and have nothing good to say about anybody.

- Live an unhealthy lifestyle by taking no exercise, drinking
  too much and eating the wrong foods.

- Work in a meaningless job with a toxic boss and toxic co-
  workers.

- Fail to live within your means by spending excessively and
  recklessly. Buy things that you want but don't really need.

HOW TO THINK YOURSELF HAPPY

Accept yourself unconditionally, warts and all. After all, nobody is perfect. To become a happy person, think happy thoughts and get rid of negative thinking. People are prone to exaggerate their problems. Nothing is as bad as you think and things are more likely to work out better than you anticipate. Nevertheless, adopt a realistic outlook. Very positive people sometimes ignore warning signals that everything is not right, particularly where their health is concerned. While anticipating the best, prepare for the worst.

"What lies behind us and what lies before us are tiny matters compared to what lies within us." – Ralph Waldo Emerson

---

Don't take responsibility for things that are not of your doing. You may do your best for people but they are ultimately responsible for their own actions and lives. Perception is important. It's not how the world is that matters, but how you see the world and how resilient you are. Viktor Frankl, in his book *The Search for Meaning* about his time spent in Nazi concentration camps, showed that we each have the ability to choose our thoughts and control our minds. Nobody can make you feel bad unless you allow them to. Sometimes it's not what happened but how you think about it that matters. See the silver lining in every cloud.

Perfection is impossible. Happy people are "satisficers" rather than "maximizers". In other words, they are prepared to accept what is good enough rather than waste time trying to constantly seek perfection. It is the paradox of choice that the availability of too many options leaves us stressed, confused and inherently unsatisfied. Irrespective of what decision we make and how good the outcome, we still feel unfulfilled because of unrealised possibilities. In fact, limiting choice doesn't just reduce anxiety, it actually makes us happier.

> **"He who has health has hope, and he who has hope has everything."** – Arabian proverb

SUMMARY

Your brain is plastic and has an insatiable appetite for learning. Change your brain by changing your ideas. Experience strengthens existing neurons and creates new ones. People may be right or left brain dominated. Those with right-dominated brains tend to be negative thinkers. Those with left-dominated brains tend to be more positive.

Happiness tends to remain stable over a lifetime. Happy children usually become happy adults. Happy people think happy thoughts, nurture happy memories and exude happiness to others. Unhappy people tend to be moaners and groaners.

You will guarantee yourself misery if you brood on your weaknesses and problems and remind yourself of your short-comings and inadequacies. To become a happy person, think happy thoughts.

Five Activities to Improve Your Happiness

1) Undertake new and challenging activities to change your brain in a positive way.

2) Pay particular attention to the positive things that happen to you each day.

3) To prevent SAD get out in the daylight in the winter for a few hours each day.

4) Seek out happy people and avoid negative people.

5) To become a happy person think happy thoughts and engage in activities that will make you happy.

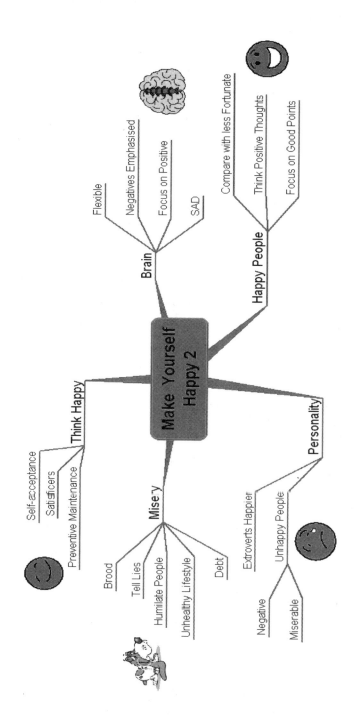

Make Yourself Happy 2

Brain
- Flexible
- Negatives Emphasised
- Focus on Positive
- SAD

Happy People
- Compare with less Fortunate
- Think Positive Thoughts
- Focus on Good Points

Think Happy
- Self-acceptance
- Satisficers
- Preventive Maintenance

Misery
- Brood
- Tell Lies
- Humilate People
- Unhealthy Lifestyle
- Debt

Personality
- Extroverts Happier
- Unhappy People
  - Negative
  - Miserable

3

FLOW

❖ *What is flow?*

❖ *Where does flow happen?*

❖ *What can you do to make flow happen?*

❖ *What is the role of memory in flow?*

❖ *How can you achieve flow at work?*

INTRODUCTION

Flow is a sense of well-being that happens when you get totally immersed in an activity by applying your skills to a challenge. Flow can be achieved through everyday mundane activities like reading, writing, gardening, exercising or doing crosswords. Memory provides a storehouse for flow experiences. Appreciate your senses by enjoying and developing the sense of seeing, hearing, tasting and movement. Flow can be experienced at work and at play.

> *"Flow with whatever may happen and let your mind be free. Stay centred by accepting whatever you are doing. This is the ultimate."* – **Chuang Tzu**

CHARACTERISTICS OF FLOW

Flow normally happens when you apply your skills to a challenging situation. The situation should be within your capabilities – not too difficult and not too easy. If the situation is too difficult it will create tension and frustration. If it is too easy it will create feelings of boredom and lack of challenge. Flow requires focused concentration and complete immersion and involvement with the present moment. There is no sense of self, as you become completely absorbed and one with the action. Flow activities are enjoyable, creating a natural high. This encourages us to persist and return to the flow activity. When the goal is achieved you can set more difficult tasks to create challenge and flow once more. During flow, time is distorted. It may seem to fly quickly or seem very long. Athletes refer to flow as being "in the zone", religious mystics describe the feeling as ecstasy, and artists and musicians get lost in the rhythm of the activity.

> *"People who learn to control inner experiences will be able to determine the quality of their lives, which is as close as any of us can come to being happy." –* **Mihaly Csikszentmihalyi**

Flow is a four-step process:

1. Identify sources of flow. Sources of flow can be found at work or recreation by applying a set of skills to a challenging situation.

2. Take action. Flow is a process with a beginning, middle and an end. Measure the progress towards your goal. Break your goals into sub-goals. Enjoyment is in the process of getting there. Achieving your goal counts for less. Make sure you enjoy the journey and savour the excitement of achieving sub-goals.

3. Allow yourself enough time. Flow is a timeless state and during the experience you will lose track of time. However

it does take time, effort and concentration to get into a state of flow.

4. Make flow a regular part of your day. Consider the ways you can enrich your day and get into a flow experience. Even housewives can experience flow as they get immersed in mundane housekeeping tasks such as cleaning and washing up and forget about the passage of time. It is not the task as much as the focused attention and interest that produces flow.

When Flow Can Occur

People often undergo flow when they are on foreign holidays because of the novelty of the experience. Flow activities are ones that you find absorbing, interesting and creative. They create moments requiring your full attention. They provide an immediate sense of reward and feedback. They come from self-knowledge – knowing what makes you unique, what gives you a sense of purpose and what makes you happy. Flow activities do not always present themselves. Sometimes you have to seek them out. A meaningful conversation with a friend may become a flow experience.

"From the beginning, what I was connecting with in the gym was a universal energy source. I would just feel it flowing. Even when I was twenty years old, I called the gym my church. When I was there, it wasn't about being social; it was about doing my practise. I was in it. I was in the zone." **– Shawn Philips**

THE ROLE OF MEMORY IN FLOW

The Greeks personified memory as Mnemosyne – the mother of the nine Muses. Mnemosyne represents the rote memorisation practised to preserve the stories of history and sagas of myth before the introduction of writing. The most prized mental gift is a well-stocked memory. With such a memory you are self-contained and autonomous. Be the historian of your own family or locality. Having knowledge of where you came from and past history is a great contributor to your quality of life. Photos are a record of past history and should be cherished. Create a photo album so that you can relish and savour the past. A well-stocked memory is a storehouse for mental flow possibilities and facilitates creativity and the solution of mental problems. Some of the best human experiences and inventions start as a simple thought. Reading is one of the most popular and accessible flow activities and is readily available and inexpensive. When absorbed in an interesting book you are likely to forget about the passage of time. Doing crossword puzzles is a mental challenge and also a great source of flow. Challenge yourself by trying to do something better than it has ever been done before. Strive to perfect your skill in the discipline that you find interesting, absorbing, challenging and rewarding. To discover what interests you move out of your comfort zone by trying something unfamiliar and different from time to time.

"The best moments in our lives are not the passive, receptive, relaxing times. The best moments usually occur if a person's body or mind is stretched to its limits in a voluntary effort to accomplish something difficult and worthwhile." – Mihaly Csikszentmihalyi

SAVOURING

Savouring is a deliberate awareness of a pleasurable experience. Savouring can be indulging in the moment such as marvelling at the beauty of a sunset or a natural landscape. It could be singing in a choir, enjoying wonderful music, indulging in the delights of a good bottle of wine, delighting in a warm shower, enjoying a hot breakfast, or tasting the flavours of your favourite dish. It could be expressing gratitude for all the good things in your life. It could be basking in the praise or congratulations of others. Happiness comes in moments so take the opportunity to relish each one.

Live each day to the fullest, since none of us know what tomorrow may bring. Don't spend too much time thinking about past or future events. Some people think their lives are really going to begin some day in the future when in fact they should be enjoying it now. This doesn't mean we shouldn't remember and learn from the past. Neither does it mean that we shouldn't plan for the future. It does mean that we should be more mindful of the present as the present is the only reality we have. Future-oriented people should consider Pascal's remark that we too often live as if the present were merely a preparation for the future. "So we never live, but we hope to live and as we are always preparing to be happy, it is inevitable we should never do so." Relish ordinary experiences and reminisce with family, friends and work colleagues about activities and past events that you enjoyed doing together. Celebrate good news and important milestones in life such as birthdays and anniversaries.

"Cultivating a generous spirit starts with mindfulness. Mindfulness, simply stated, means paying attention to what is actually happening; it's about what is really going on." **– Nell Newman**

Appreciate and use your senses, such as sight, hearing, taste and touch. Be open to beauty and excellence in the world around you. Appreciate works of art. Visual art has a history and is imbued with the emotions, values, hopes and ideas of the painter. Train your sight to take a sensory delight in seeing. The joy of movement can be experienced through dance. You don't need to be a professional dancer to enjoy yourself. Dance can be a great source of flow by allowing you to get totally involved in the rhythm while at the same time keeping fit and healthy. The joys of movement can also be experienced through miming and acting.

We are genetically programmed for sex. Nevertheless, some of us have been programmed by parents, religious beliefs and society to have all sorts of inhibitions about sex. Relax and savour the joys of sex and love in a committed relationship as it can be a most compelling and rewarding experience.

FLOW AT PLAY

There are great opportunities for flow at play provided you plan your recreational pursuits. Most of us spend our free time at activities such as watching television, reading, conversing with friends, hobbies, going to restaurants, cinema, theatre or the more vigorous and physically fit get involved in sport. It is estimated, however, that most people spend four times more time watching television than doing sports or hobbies. This is despite the fact that watching television is the least likely activity to create happiness and flow in your life. You should identify those activities which you enjoy doing most as they are the ones likely to create flow.

"People are at their most mindful when they are at play. If we find ways of enjoying our work blurring the lines between work and play the gains will be greater." – **Ellen Langer**

Many people who developed interests outside work such as writing, art, music, poetry, gardening, cooking or invention have gone on to win renown in their chosen fields. Such people often make an invaluable contribution to their country's literature and culture. The only difference between these people and others who squander their time is the attention, energy, enthusiasm and commitment they give to their interests. Even at the time of the Industrial Revolution, when people worked more than 80 hours per week, some found time for cultural pursuits such as poetry and literature rather than wasting their time in pubs.

FLOW AT WORK

Historically, work has got a bad press. The Industrial Revolution and the scientific management approach took the joy out of work. The Bible teaches us that God punished Adam for his ambition by sentencing him to work the earth with the sweat of his brow. It's no wonder that the average person sees work as a chore rather than a potential source of satisfaction and joy. Many people consider jobs as something they have to do – a burden imposed from outside and not contributing to their long-term goals. It's just seen as a way of earning money and putting bread on the table.

> *"It does not seem to be true that work necessarily needs to be unpleasant. It may always have to be hard, or at least harder than doing nothing at all. But there is ample evidence that work can be enjoyable, and that indeed, it is often the most enjoyable part of life." – Mihaly Csikszentmihalyi*

However, in the post-industrial world work is becoming more enjoyable again. Managers now realise the importance of job satisfaction and a happy workforce to increased productivity in the workplace. We spend a large part of our time making a living so if we can find flow in work it will be worthwhile and make us happier. Balance between work and play is important to finding flow in all areas of your life, however.

Doing Work that You Enjoy Creates Flow

Generally, there are more opportunities for flow at work than elsewhere, even though most people think otherwise. Happiness is achieved when you accomplish something, especially if it was difficult to do. To create flow identify your natural strengths such as persistence, logic, creativity, enthusiasm, appreciation of beauty and love of learning and choose work where you can use them, preferably in the service of something greater than you are. You are more likely to value a job, relationship or hobby that aligns and uses your core signature strengths.

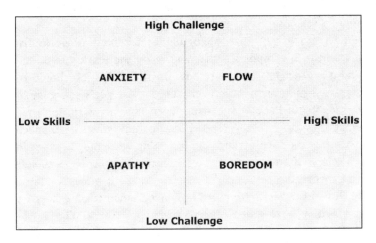

High Challenge

ANXIETY | **FLOW**

Low Skills ——————————————— **High Skills**

APATHY | **BOREDOM**

Low Challenge

Figure 1: Csikszentmihalyi Flow Model

In your job you may need to redesign work to accommodate your signature strengths. Flow is more likely if the work provides a challenge and you are trying to achieve targets and goals. It is important that your signature strengths are matched to the challenge. Jobs that offer little challenge are boring and those with too much challenge can be stressful. Ones in between that are challenging but not too demanding provide optimal flow. You may need to experiment with different jobs to find the one that suits you and provides flow. Generally, work that requires higher qualifications and higher levels of skill are more satisfying.

> "**Work is either fun or drudgery. It depends on your attitude. I like fun.**" – Colleen C. Barrett

Even routine work can provide opportunities for flow. Adopt a philosophy of continuous improvement by looking at operations that could be streamlined. Are there ways in which the work can be done more efficiently? Could operations be eliminated or combined to improve the flow of work? If people spent more time trying to improve the work and less time trying to avoid it they would be happier and create more opportunities for flow.

As there are more opportunities for flow at work than elsewhere, it's important that you enjoy the work you do and find it meaningful. To create flow possibilities, a job should resemble a game with variety, challenge, clear goals and immediate feedback. People who experience flow at work don't feel what they do is really work because they enjoy it so much. They feel they are getting paid for doing what they love to do. They are often able to change constraints into opportunities and change the context of the job to make it more conducive to flow. Managers have more flow experiences than others because they have more control over their work. Those who don't experience flow at work are doing jobs they don't enjoy or find meaningful. The reasons for dissatisfaction include lack of variety and challenge, conflict, boredom and burnout.

SUMMARY

You create flow by using your skills in a challenging situation. You don't have to be a great athlete to have a flow experience. Ordinary everyday activities like reading, writing and gardening can create them. A well-stocked memory can be the source of mental flow experiences.

Don't postpone happiness. Happiness occurs in moments and you should savour each one. The senses provide great opportunities for flow. Develop your sense of sight, hearing, taste and movement. You don't have to be a professional to experience the joy and flow of dance.

There are more opportunities for flow at work than anywhere else. People find flow in work that they enjoy doing and find challenging. The reasons for dissatisfaction at work include lack of variety and challenge, conflict, boredom and burnout.

Five Activities to Create Flow

1) The next time you read try to focus your concentration on the text eliminating all mental and external distractions. Choose a book about a topic that will absorb and interest you.

2) Move out of your comfort zone by trying something challenging, unfamiliar and different such as learning a new skill or going on a foreign holiday.

3) Notice the way music is used to create atmosphere and experience the effects. Get lost in the flow. It can be used to create solemnity at a funeral and feelings of joy at a wedding. National anthems are used to create feelings of patriotism and national pride.

4) The next time you are dancing get into the flow by losing yourself in the rhythm.

5) Try to create flow opportunities at work. Pretend the job is a challenging game with variety, clear goals, constant feedback and possibilities for improvement and thus create a self-fulfilling prophecy.

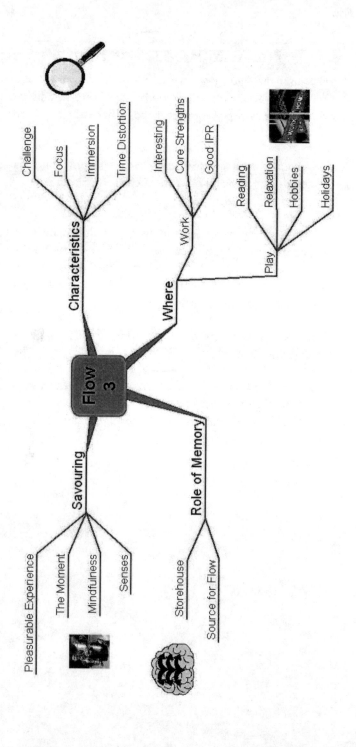

Flow
3

Characteristics
- Challenge
- Focus
- Immersion
- Time Distortion

Where
- Work
  - Interesting
  - Core Strengths
  - Good IPR
- Play
  - Reading
  - Relaxation
  - Hobbies
  - Holidays

Savouring
- Pleasurable Experience
- The Moment
- Mindfulness
- Senses

Role of Memory
- Storehouse
- Source for Flow

4

MONEY AND HAPPINESS

- ❖ *Does money buy happiness?*
- ❖ *What are the effects of materialism?*
- ❖ *Why does money matter?*
- ❖ *What is reference anxiety?*
- ❖ *Has more wealth made countries happier?*

INTRODUCTION

Having more than you need is not a recipe for happiness. Over-indulgence and being in debt brings unhappiness, anxiety and stress. Individualism, materialism and greed are the dominant philosophies of developed economies. Economists measure wealth as increases in gross national production or more consumption rather than increases in happiness. It would be naïve to think that money is irrelevant. It provides you with a descent standard of living and gives many benefits like independence, security of mind and freedom from financial worries. Celebrity and fame may bring misery rather than happiness. In contrast, people who live a simple lifestyle are often happy. Many people suffer from "reference anxiety" or the desire to keep up with the Joneses. Extra income makes more difference to happiness in poorer countries than in richer ones. Happiness rises as people are lifted out of extreme poverty and are able to afford the basic necessities of life. In the developed world, depression, alcoholism, obesity, suicide and crime have risen in pace with rising standards of living since World War II.

DOES MONEY BUY HAPPINESS?

On a personal level money does not buy much more happiness beyond a relatively low threshold of wealth. In general, those who strongly desire and pursue wealth are unhappier than those who do not. Those on a high income are likely to spend more time at work and commuting, and less time at leisure or with their family. It seems having more than you need is not a recipe for happiness. Accumulating income and possessions may only add to your worries as the more you have the more you want. Happiness is provided more by the anticipation of owning a house or a car rather than the actual acquisition. You get another boost of happiness when you buy them, but then you quickly get used to them.

Once you're able to afford life's necessities, more and more money provides diminishing returns in terms of happiness. Money does produce happiness if the increased income lifts you from poverty into middle class. On the other hand, it does not necessarily guarantee happiness if it allows you to upgrade your lifestyle from one that is merely comfortable to one that is luxurious. Inheriting a fortune or winning the lottery doesn't necessarily bring long-term happiness. People who inherit wealth or win the lottery adapt and return to their previous level of happiness within a few years. While money may not bring happiness, it is unlikely to cause misery.

> *"Those who seek happiness in pleasure, wealth, glory, power, and heroics are as naïve as the child who tries to catch a rainbow and wear it as a coat."* **– Delgo Kyhentse Renpoche**

Research in 2008 by two Wharton economists, Professors Wolfers and Stevenson, suggests that as countries get richer their inhabitants become happier. Economic gains bring better food, clothing, housing, medical care and a longer life which result in substantial increases in happiness. Their findings challenge the conventional wisdom of the past three decades, which held that higher national gross domestic product often doesn't translate into a greater overall sense of well-being and happiness. Although within countries happiness does increase with wealth, it tends to slow down once a certain level of prosperity has been achieved. Once poverty, hunger, thirst and fear of violence have gone, rises in average prosperity have no effect on average levels of happiness. This is known as the Easterlin Paradox, named after Richard Easterlin's findings as set out in his 1974 paper titled "Does Economic Growth Improve the Human Lot?"

"The gross national product does not allow for the health of our children, the quality of their education, or the joy of their play. It does not include the beauty of our poetry or the strength of our marriages; the intelligence of our public debate or the integrity of our public officials. It measures neither our wit nor our courage; neither our wisdom nor our learning; neither our compassion nor our devotion to our country; it measures everything, in short, except that which makes life worthwhile." – **Robert F. Kennedy**

Sufficient is Enough

Most people are happy if they have sufficient income to live a comfortable life. Surveys show that those living in upper income households are more likely to be satisfied with their lives and happier than those in middle and lower income households. However, having highly educated parents is a stronger predictor of happiness than income as they act as good role models. Wealth is like health – absence breeds misery but having it doesn't necessarily guarantee happiness. To be happy it is important to live within your means. Being in debt brings anxiety and stress. Money matters more to some than to others as different people have different priorities. In fact, the more a person values money the less satisfied they are when they acquire it. Some people love their work irrespective of the money they earn. To them job satisfaction and enjoying good interpersonal relationships at work is more important than money.

In 1930 the famous economist John Maynard Keynes thought that affluence would bring more leisure time. Riches would liberate people from toil to enjoy the finer things in life. In more recent times, with the emergence of labour-saving devices and the information and communications revolution, it was thought that people would not need to work the long hours they used to. Instead, people are working harder and longer in order to afford the things that they think will make them happy – bigger houses, bigger cars, bigger televisions and foreign holidays. They are upwardly mobile and yearn to have greater status and outward signs of wealth. They thus tend to buy designer clothes, eat in the best restaurants and send their children to private schools.

"Annual income twenty pounds, annual expenditure nineteen pounds and six pence, result happiness. Annual income twenty pounds, annual expenditure twenty pounds and six pence, result misery." – **Charles Dickens**

Since 1949 real income has doubled in the USA while happiness has not risen proportionately. This is despite increased leisure time, better health, longer life spans and a decline in racial and gender inequality. It seems higher income brings higher aspiration and expectation levels, rather than higher happiness levels. Similarly, people in Western Europe enjoy a higher standard of living but yet are not happier, although they are happier than people in poorer nations. Within a particular country the better off report themselves to be more satisfied than the poor, but it is relative rather than absolute incomes that seem to matter. In the West the rise in the standard of living has been accompanied by an increase in depression, drug use, alcoholism, obesity, suicide, crime and divorce. The Institute of Psychiatry in 2007 reported that the number of children with emotional and behavioural problems in the UK has doubled in the last 25 years. The number of adolescent suicides has quadrupled and younger people account for more than their share of road deaths. Many people in the West live alone and are lonely. According to Sigmund Freud, the price we pay for our advance in civilisation is a loss of happiness.

Less Community Spirit

Individualism, consumerism and materialism are the dominant philosophy in the modern developed society giving rise to selfishness and greed. Increased mobility and incivility has brought crime and indifference to the needs of others. People often no longer spend sufficient time in a locality to lay down roots, get to know each other and form friendships. Getting involved in local community groups is a thing of the past as most people haven't the time or the energy to do so after putting in a long day at work. The spare time they have is used up watching television. Work is all consuming while family life and friendships are neglected.

> **"All I want is a chance to prove that money can't make me happy." – Spike Milligan**

SIMPLE LIFESTYLE AND HAPPINESS

Amish people in the USA live frugally and are by all accounts very happy. They have a great sense of community spirit. They reject all modernisation and prefer to live a simple traditional way of life. They are a model of humility in an egotistical world. The box-like style of Amish buggies is symbolic of the lack of pretension in Amish life. Rubber tyres are not permitted. They wear simple, standardised clothes symbolising humility and loyalty to the community.

The Maasai of South Africa live traditional tribal lives without the comforts of modern living and are still happy. Surveys show that deprived and malnourished children living in the slums of Calcutta and Manila can be happy despite enduring extreme poverty. Tribespeople in the Amazon jungle are happy without the benefits of western comforts. Jose "Pepe" Alvarez, an ex-friar in the Order of St Augustine in Spain but who now works with the Peruvian Amazon Research Institute, maintains that these people are happier than people in the US and Europe. People in the West have more possessions but also more worries and less peace of mind and happiness than many people who live a simple life in the jungle. Their key to happiness is enjoying simple things and every moment as it comes, and not worrying too much about the past or future. It seems that material wealth is not a basic psychological need, while relating to others is.

"It is not how much we have, but how much we enjoy, that makes happiness." – **Charles Spurgeon**

A 2006 New Economics Foundation/Friends of the Earth survey shows that Vanuatu (pop. 200,000), an island in the South Pacific, is the happiest place on earth using criteria such as life expectancy, human well-being and environmental damage despite being a subsistence economy. It seems people are happy in Vanuatu because they are satisfied with very little. It is not a consumer-driven society. Life in Vanuatu is about community, family and goodwill to other people.

DOES MONEY BUY LOVE?

A 2004 survey by the National Bureau of Economic Research at Massachusetts has for the first time made a link between wealth, happiness and sex. It surveyed 16,000 Americans asking them personal questions about their bank balances and love lives. They concluded that greater income does not buy more sex, or sexual partners. In fact, they found that unemployed people tend to have more sex and more sexual partners than people who are gainfully employed. However, sex isn't everything as unemployed people have higher rates of depression and are not as happy as the general population. The survey found that sex is the thing that makes us happiest, with the highly educated more likely to find ultimate pleasure from sex than those with fewer academic qualifications.

"An intellectual is someone who has found something more interesting than sex." – **Edgar Wallace**

WHEN MONEY MATTERS

It would be naive to think that money does not matter. Money gives you many benefits. It gives you independence, security of mind and freedom from financial pressures and worries. You have the freedom to travel anywhere in the world and you can buy your own home. You can send your children to the best schools and you can help your family financially to give them a good start in life. You can pay skilled people to do DIY jobs around the house. When you are sick you can avail of the best medical services. If you feel you have too much money you can off load some of it by becoming a philanthropist and donating money to worthwhile causes.

Research shows that money spent on experiences such as holidays, concerts and night outs brings more joy than money spent on physical goods. It seems the things that don't last create the most happiness. If the experience is a holiday, for instance, you will maximise your level of happiness by savouring the planning and anticipation of the event. Read guidebooks and surf the web to find out all you need to know about your destination. You'll find that you can enjoy the whole process of planning the holiday as much as the holiday itself. In addition, the memories created by holidays can be recalled as often as you like and even mentally edited, embellished and elaborated to eliminate any bad experiences. Memories of experiences shared are often the glue that keeps relationships and friendships intact and we know that these make a huge contribution to our happiness.

"It's good to have money and the things that money can buy, but it's good, too, to check up once in a while and make sure that you haven't lost the things that money can't buy." – **George Horace Lorimer**

Some Comparisons Are Invidious

Comparing ourselves with those who are better off may engender feelings of envy and resentment. The idea that happiness is a function of the gap between what we have and what we think others have goes all the way back to Aristotle. However, no matter how rich you are wealth comparisons with others can make you unhappy. There are always people better off than you. The trick is to compare yourself with the less wealthy and to be happy with what you have. If one's neighbour earns more than you do, then you may feel less happy than if the neighbour earned less. Living in a rich neighbourhood and being surrounded by people who are wealthier than you could be detrimental to your health. On the other hand, being a big fish in a small pond may be advantageous as it makes you feel comparatively important and well-off. Since people's happiness is affected by relative rather than actual income, governments could arguably increase the happiness quotient of the population by simply using an increase in income taxes to redistribute wealth.

Many people suffer from what psychologists call "reference anxiety". It's the modern form of "keeping up with the Joneses". People judge their status in comparison with others and are often prepared to get into debt to keep up with them. One study found the richer people were relative to their peers, the happier they tended to be. We have rising expectations constantly fed by advertisements and exposure to the rich and famous on television, celebrity magazines, tabloid newspapers and the internet. People don't realise that for most of us this is fantasy land rather than reality.

> **"Money may be the husk of many things but not the kernel.** *It brings you food, but not appetite; medicine, but not health; acquaintance, but not friends; servants, but not loyalty; days of joy, but not peace or happiness."* – Henrik Ibsen

We know, however, that fame and wealth in itself does not bring happiness. Many famous stars have died from alcohol and drug abuse after years fighting addiction and leading troublesome lives. Psychologists believe that enormous success is healthy only for people with a high level of self-esteem. For those struggling with a poor self-image, coping with too much success can bring many problems. The average person is able to cope with success when it is more modest and gradual and they have the maturity to handle it.

COMPARING COUNTRIES

In affluent countries 85 to 90 per cent of people report that they are either happy or very happy. The people who are unhappy are the unemployed and the mentally ill. Different happiness surveys give different results depending on the criteria used and some have even placed Nigeria as the world's happiest country with Mexico a strong second. Extra income makes more difference to happiness in poorer countries than in richer ones. Happiness rises as people are lifted out of poverty and achieve a reasonable standard of living.

Additional income beyond a certain level is not associated with additional happiness in developed countries. It seems extra happiness declines steadily as one gets richer. However, richer people are on average happier than poorer people in the same country, but this is largely because people compare their incomes with other people in their society. The former communist countries are the unhappiest of all. It seems democracy is not an instant solution to happiness for people used to an environment of spying, control, suspicion, secrecy, surveillance and lack of respect for human rights. People must develop the faith and confidence to trust each other before they can become happy. People are no happier in the USA even though they are much better off. This is despite the fact that Americans consider happiness more important to them than money, moral goodness and even going to Heaven. There is a similar story in Britain and Japan. The picture is slightly different in Europe. Happiness is slightly up in Italy whereas in Belgium it is sharply down.

"Happiness, whether for us or for our children, is not the result of earthly riches, which must either be lost by us in our lifetime or else must pass after our death into the possession of those we do not know or, it may be, of those whom we do not wish to have them. It is God who gives happiness; for he is the true wealth of men's souls." – **Saint Augustine (354-430 AD)**

The high-taxed Nordic countries like Denmark, Norway and Sweden, where there is a clearer vision of the common good and developed welfare systems, are among the happiest. This is in line with the ideas of the late J.K. Galbraith as expressed in his book, *The Affluent Society*. He suggested that too many productive resources are devoted to goods which ultimately do not contribute to the quality of life, unlike public expenditure on education and healthcare which do. In fact, surveys over 30 years show the Danes score higher than any other Western country on measures of life satisfaction, even if they pay high levels of tax. It is a well-structured, well-ordered society with decent housing, a good health service and a cheap efficient public transport system. It spends more per capita on children and the elderly than any other country in the world. Ninety-two per cent of Danes belong to some sort of social club. Levels of trust in the Nordic countries are much higher than anywhere else in the world. Similarly, Canada, with a good health system, comes out near the top in ratings of happiness.

> **"I want chancellors of the exchequer and chief finance officers to buy into this research about happiness. I think it is our challenge to demonstrate that there is good science now to help us help people have better lives."** – Richard Reeves

In 2004 and 2006, the *Economist* ranked Ireland's "quality of life" as the best in the world. It would be interesting to see what the current recession will have on the result. After centuries of persecution, misfortune and even famine, Ireland has at last an enviable life style and earning power. Even in sport, music and literature the Irish seem to be on a high. However, the emergence of malpractice and corruption in the banking sector has diminished the reputation of Ireland in the eyes of the world's financial community. One major bank has been nationalised and the other two main banks have been recapitalised leaving the Irish taxpayer exposed to a high financial risk. The national budget is in deficit and attempts by the Government to rectify the situation by introducing a pension levy on public sector employees have seen them taking to the streets in protest.

Social psychologists who measured the three predictors of well-being – wealth, education and health – found that countries with large populations like China, Japan and India tend to have lower levels of happiness than smaller countries with greater social cohesion and a stronger sense of national identity like Denmark and Switzerland. Surveys consistently show that the unhappiest countries in the world are from the former communist countries of the Soviet Union and the East European bloc like Russia, Romania, Albania, Lithuania, Estonia, Latvia, Belarus, Bulgaria and the Ukraine. Political instability also lowers happiness.

Gross National Happiness

Economists place little emphasis on how happy people are. They measure progress by rises in gross national product on the assumption that if people consume more they are better off. However, there have been some attempts at measurement. Erasmus University in Rotterdam runs a World Database of Happiness, and the tiny country of Bhutan has established a Gross National Happiness (GNH) index based on the Buddhist idea that economic growth alone does not bring happiness. In Bhutan happiness is pursued as a conscious national goal. Bhutan's GNH has four pillars generally in line with the emerging field of happiness studies. These are sustainable and equitable socio-economic development, conservation of the environment, preservation and promotion of culture and good governance. According to a national census in 2005, nearly 97 per cent of their population said they were either "happy" or "very happy", while the country's GDP is now higher than most neighbouring countries. In many developed countries there is an underinvestment in the health system. It seems that governments do not realise the importance of health to the general well-being and happiness of their citizens. Countries with good public health systems tend to top the happiness charts.

"The accumulation of material goods is at an all-time high, but so is the number of people who feel emptiness in their lives." – **Al Gore**

SUMMARY

Money does not buy happiness beyond a threshold of wealth sufficient to meet our needs. Accumulating wealth and possessions may only add to your worries. Amish people in the USA live frugally and are very happy mainly because of their sense of community. Since 1949 real income has doubled in the USA while happiness has declined a little. People in the developed world enjoy a higher standard of living but are not happier. Individualism and materialism is the dominant philosophy in the modern developed world. This gives rise to selfishness and greed.

It would be naïve to think that money does not matter. Money gives many benefits including independence, security of mind and freedom from financial worries. Wealth generally brings more prestige and status, though rich and famous people are not necessarily happy. Many people suffer from what psychologists call 'reference anxiety'. People judge their possessions in comparison with others and are often prepared to go into debt to keep up with them. Extra income makes more difference to happiness in poorer countries than in richer ones. Happiness rises as people are lifted out of extreme poverty. Their health also improves because of better sanitation and housing. Economists place little emphasis on how happy people are. They measure progress by rises in gross national product on the assumption that if people consume more they are better off. Rises in standards of living in the developed world has been accompanied by a rise in criminality.

Five Activities to Improve Your Happiness

1) Balance your budget each week. Ensure you live within your means. Being in debt brings anxiety, stress and unhappiness. It also means the stress of unwelcome calls from debt collectors!

2) Volunteer to do work for a local community group or charity. As well as making you happy it will occupy your spare time productively and create friendships.

3) Be courteous, kind and mannerly to all you meet. It doesn't cost anything and it will make you and the person you meet happier.

4) Simplify your lifestyle. Remove the clutter from your life. Give away the things to charity that you don't really need.

5) Visit an elderly person in your area. They will appreciate the gesture and it will make you and the person you visit happier.

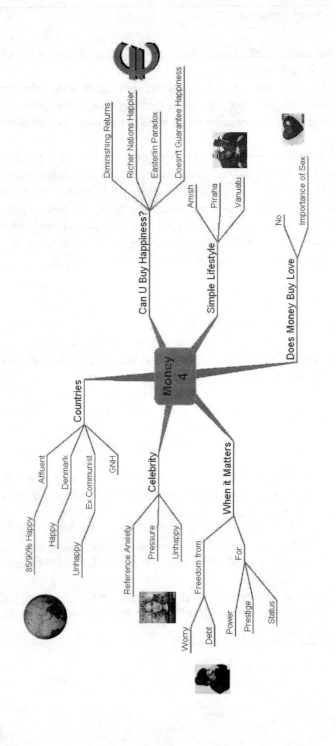

Money 4

Can U Buy Happiness?
- Diminishing Returns
- Richer Nations Happier
- Easterlin Paradox
- Doesn't Guarantee Happiness

Simple Lifestyle
- Amish
- Piraha
- Vanuatu

Does Money Buy Love
- No
- Importance of Sex

Countries
- 85/90% Happy — Affluent
- Happy — Denmark
- Unhappy — Ex Communist
- GNH

Celebrity
- Reference Anxiety
- Pressure
- Unhappy

When it Matters
- Freedom from
  - Worry
  - Debt
- For
  - Power
  - Prestige
  - Status

5

RELATIONSHIPS

- ❖ *Why are friendships important?*
- ❖ *Why are married couples happier?*
- ❖ *Why is empathy so important?*
- ❖ *What can you do to nurture friendship?*

INTRODUCTION

Good relationships are an important source for happiness. Over a lifetime we make hundreds of friends but only a few of these will last and become close.

Relationships are nurtured by love and displays of affection. They are undermined by contempt and constant criticism. Married couples are happier than single people or cohabiting couples. Divorced, separated and widowed people may be unhappy for many years after the event. Criticism, contempt, defensiveness and stonewalling are the signs of a deteriorating situation in a marriage.

Widowed people may never fully recover from the death of a spouse although they are likely eventually to return to a reasonable level of happiness. Empathy can be emotional or rational and is an important skill in maintaining sound relationships. Trust is an important aspect of friendship. Self-confidence will help you make friends easily. Men and women differ in the way they relate and handle emotions.

> *"He who has so little knowledge of human nature as to seek happiness by changing anything but his own disposition will waste his life in fruitless effort."* – Dr. Johnson

INTERPERSONAL RELATIONSHIPS

Relationships are the most important source of happiness. Develop the skill of unconditional love by loving people for who they really are and not for what you want them to be. Don't be judgemental. Everybody is unique and we all have different ways of reacting and doing things. Accept their faults as none of us are perfect. On the dark side, many life problems are caused by poor social relationships. In every relationship there are bound to be some issues, conflict and differences of opinion. Insisting on your own way is not a recipe for good relationships.

Remain flexible by keeping talking and compromising as needed. Be slow to take offence and quick to forgive and forget. Refuse to react to innuendo, provocation and sarcastic remarks. Adding fuel to the fire only makes things worse. Don't ever intentionally set out to stir up trouble and provoke people. Don't be governed by your ego and get stuck in a particular point of view even if you are convinced you're right. Develop traits of humility and consideration rather than be full of your own importance. People should develop common interests and shared goals to help their relationships along.

Most adults claim that friendship is more important than career, money or family. Even children put friendship in the number two position after family, highlighting that close personal relationships are still the most important elements in their young lives. One in three people meet their friends at work and some even meet their future partners there. Men on average have fewer friends than women. They tend to have acquaintances rather than friends. Even women have less regular contact with friends because of the need to juggle family and work responsibilities. People who are fortunate to have friends or social support are healthier and visit their doctor less.

> "Don't flatter yourself that friendship authorises you to say disagreeable things to your intimates. The nearer you come into relation with a person, the more necessary do tact and courtesy become. Except in cases of necessity, which are rare, leave your friend to learn unpleasant things from his enemies; they are ready enough to tell him." – Oliver Wendell Holmes

PARTNERS

Accept and appreciate your partner's love. Realise that you and your partner are different and that you both have your own particular needs. Stay in touch with reality by not projecting unrealistic expectations or fantasies on your partner. Sometimes we project our own failings, shortcomings and inadequacies on to others.

Have plenty of physical contact with your partner. Touch is the language of love including sex, caresses and cuddles. Every day do something together that you enjoy. This can be something as simple as going for a walk together. Break the routine by going away for a few days for a romantic break in a hotel or go for an intimate meal in a nice restaurant. This will refresh and invigorate your relationship. To love others you must love yourself. Loving yourself develops from self-knowledge and feelings of self-esteem and self-acceptance. This means accepting that you are not perfect, but behind the imperfections is a good person who wants to improve and learn from their mistakes.

Happiness starts with love and displays of affection. Always communicate your love to your partner in both words and deeds. Give support and build up your partner's self-esteem by showing your appreciation for what they do in your life. Don't make unfavourable comparisons with others as you may undermine your partner's self-image and self-confidence.

> *"If one is estranged from oneself, then one is es-*
> *tranged from others too. If one is out of touch with*
> *oneself, then one cannot touch others."* – **Anne Mor-**
> **row Lindbergh**

MARRIAGE

A *New Scientist* magazine study in 2003 found that there is a clear boost to happiness from marriage. It lasts from about a year before a couple's wedding until a year afterwards. Although satisfaction levels tend to diminish in later years, a happy prolonged marriage has a permanent positive effect. The *Irish Times*/TNS mrbi 2006 poll found that the married over-50s enjoyed physical and psychological health. They enjoy a better quality of life and suffer less anxiety or depression, compared to single and divorced, separated or widowed people. The manner in which couples resolve emotionally charged conflicts predicts marital satisfaction throughout married life. Older couples appear to derive more pleasure than pain from their marriages and also show more displays of affection during conflict than do younger couples. If you think that several sexual partners over time add to the spice of life, then you are mistaken. According to an exhaustive study published in the *Social Organisation of Sexuality* (University of Chicago Press, 1994), married people have more sex than singles and more orgasms.

Persistence may be one of the secrets of happy marriages. During the 1950s, demographer Paul Glick found that high school dropouts were more likely than graduates to be divorced, leading to speculation that people who give up on some difficult things, like finishing school, are also unlikely to persevere in marriage as well. This is now known as the Glick Effect.

Married people are less likely to commit suicide. They enjoy safe and better sex and live longer. It's reputed to add seven years to the life of a man and about four years to the life of a woman. Unmarried people are at greater risk of depression. The quality of the marriage is of prime importance. People who say their marriage is satisfying, who are still in love with their partner and consider them their best friend, rarely report being unhappy, discontented with life or depressed.

Apart from the security, love and comfort of a happy marriage, married couples share resources and expertise and thus reap economies of scale. There is thus some truth in the adage that two can live as cheaply as one. Also, married people generally have better and more secure jobs and higher standards of living. People stay together in a marriage when the advantages of doing so outweigh the trauma of separation.

> *"It is not a lack of love, but a lack of friendship that makes unhappy marriages."* – **Friedrich Nietzsche**

The Key to a Successful Marriage

One marriage counsellor has put forward a magic ratio of five to one as the key to a successful marriage. This means that as long as there is five times as much positive feeling and interaction between husband and wife as there is negative, the marriage is likely to be harmonious. This would suggest that couples should accentuate the positive rather than the negative as few appreciate a nagging partner. Concentrate on the good things in your marriage rather than highlighting the bad. Nobody likes their weaknesses to be highlighted all the time. Couples need to create a secure base from which to go out into the world. This is a base in which they can be themselves and be accepted with all their shortcomings and vulnerabilities. We all need comfort, contact, connection and caring and if these needs are not being met we are likely to seek them elsewhere.

However, marriage is not a guarantee of happiness as is testified by the high rate of divorce in the western world. The least happy people are those trapped in an unhappy marriage. It causes long-term resentment when people stay in an unhappy marriage from a sense of duty. Some couples may stay together until the children grow into adults. In the meantime, continuous bickering between the parents creates an unhappy and stressful atmosphere for the children to grow up in. Thus separation may be the best option in certain circumstances. Divorced, separated and widowed people may be unhappy for many years after the event. In fact, divorced, separated, or widowed are significantly less happy than those who never married. It is more likely that people with compatible backgrounds and similar interests and personalities will be happier and stay together.

"To keep your marriage brimming,
With love in the loving cup,
Whenever you're wrong admit it;
Whenever you're right shut up." – Ogden Nash

It is more likely that positive, happy people more readily form stable, permanent and happy marriages. Happy people are more fun to be with and are more outgoing, trusting, compassionate, and focused on others. Nobody wants to be around people who are irritable, miserable, complaining and withdrawn all the time. A good marriage like a good friendship involves self-disclosure on either side. As a relationship deepens, self-disclosure increases.

Signs of a Deteriorating Relationship

Some of the signs of a deteriorating relationship include criticism, sarcasm, contempt, defensiveness and stonewalling. Each of these is more progressively damaging than the previous one.

- **Criticism**. There is a difference between criticism and complaining. Criticism involves attacking someone's personality or character rather than complaining about a specific behaviour or action. Complaining can be healthy for a marriage provided the complaints are taken on board and something is done to rectify the offending behaviour. Expressing annoyance and disagreement can make a marriage stronger rather than suppressing the complaint. Criticism can become pervasive in a marriage and create a downward spiral as it demoralises without correcting the situation that it condemns. Learning how to react in a calm way will help prevent unproductive fighting and help to solve problems in a mutually satisfactory way.

- **Contempt.** Contempt is a powerful feeling of dislike toward somebody so that you consider them worthless, inferior or undeserving of respect. Contempt is probably one of the main reasons for marriage breakdown. People showing contempt for another make that person feel humiliated, embarrassed, rejected and demeaned. They undermine another's confidence by insensitively highlighting faults, shortcomings or idiosyncrasies in front of other people. Contempt is a kind of psychological abuse and is expressed through words, deeds and body language. Research shows that people in contemptuous relationships are more likely to suffer from viral infections such as flu and colds than other people. Contempt attacks the immune system while fondness and admiration are antidotes.

"All married couples should learn the art of battle, as they should learn the art of making love. Good battle is objective and honest – never vicious or cruel. Good battle is healthy and constructive, and brings to a marriage the principle of equal partnership." – **Ann Landers**

- **Defensiveness.** Defensiveness is a natural reaction to contempt. Defensiveness may include denying responsibility, refusing to see your partner's point of view, making excuses or meeting your partner's criticism with one of your own. Being defensive is only adding to your marital problems. Learn to listen in a non-defensive way to defuse sources of difference. Instead of attacking or ignoring your partner's point of view, try to see the problem from their perspective and admit that it may have some validity. Being open and receptive will disarm your partner and make it less likely that they will continue to criticise or react with contempt towards you. An affectionate hug may prove an effective antidote.

- **Stonewalling**. This is the process of replacing communication with a stony cold silence. Stonewalling conveys disap-
  proval, disinterest and distance. It is a type of sensory deprivation as most people are gregarious and love to touch and
  talk to each other. If you cannot share your feelings and concerns an important part of your being is excluded from the
  relationship. Stonewalling is likely to induce feelings of emptiness and loneliness in a relationship. It is at this stage that
  the services of marriage counsellors are called upon and
  even then it may be too late to save the marriage.

---

*"True humour springs not more from the head than
from the heart. It is not contempt; its essence is love.
It issues not in laughter, but in still smiles, which lie
far deeper."* – **Thomas Carlyle**

WHY GOOD RELATIONSHIPS MATTER

Close relationships make us feel good and happy about ourselves. Unconditional love allows us to love and be loved. We
feel accepted, secure and safe in the relationship and this con-
tributes to our emotional well-being. The empathy and emotional support we get from others can help us get through the
inevitable trials and tribulations of life.

You know who your friends really are in times of tragedy
like personal trauma or bereavement. A good indicator of
friendship might be who visits you when you are sick in hospital. Psychological wealth is more important to our well-being
and mental health than material wealth. Psychological wealth is
increased when we are the recipients of positive communication, appreciation and kindness.

It is a good idea to be on good terms with your next door
neighbour. It is a really nice feeling to know that the people
next door are willing to help you if the need arises. You never
know when you may need their help in an emergency or to
keep a friendly eye on your house during your absence. There
is nothing worse than being on poor terms with your

neighbour as it puts you in an invidious position. The close proximity means it is hard to avoid them and trying to avoid eye contact with them can become a bit of a chore. It is a sad reflection on modern life when people don't know the people next door. In many cases the sense of community where neighbours kept a concerned eye out for each other and their children is gone. A safe supportive community is a great source of comfort and happiness.

EMPATHY

Empathy is an important part of good relationships. Empathy can be considered emotional or rational. Emotional empathy is a form of emotional validation. You get across the impression that you sincerely feel the other person's pain and know what it's like to be the other person. This takes great sensitivity and compassion. On the other hand, rational empathy is viewing the experience through the other person's eyes. Maslow said that self-actualisers had strong feelings of empathy and affection for all human beings. They had the capacity for greater love, deeper friendship and more complete identification with others than those who are not self-actualised. To derive happiness from being helpful to others, one must be able to take another's perspective, understand their feelings, and influence them in a positive way.

"There is nothing we like to see so much as the gleam of pleasure in a person's eye when he feels that we have sympathised with him, understood him. At these moments something fine and spiritual passes between two friends. These are the moments worth living."–
Don Marquis

To practise empathy you must accept that other people see things differently. Their viewpoint is shaped by unique experiences, temperament and upbringing. You literally have to get inside their head and walk in their shoes to see how they perceive the world. To be on the same waveband as other people you must be open-minded, considerate, courteous, respectful, attentive and an active listener. Take turns to discuss and make sure you do most of the listening. The reason we have two ears and one mouth is because we should listen twice as much as we talk. A sympathetic ear is half the battle. Showing contempt for another's viewpoint is the opposite of practising empathy.

HOW TO BE A BETTER FRIEND

Aristotle divided friendship into three types:

1. The first is based on brief pleasure, favoured by the young.

2. The second is based on utility, typically involving commercial transactions and are often temporary.

3. The third is perfect friendship which is based on goodness. This type of friendship is rare and needs time and intimacy to flourish. Once it does, though, it is permanent. To quote from Aristotle, "It is those who desire the good of their friends for the friends' sake that are most truly friends, because each loves the other for what he is and not for any incidental quality."

"I've learned that all a person has in life is family and friends. If you lose those you have nothing, so friends are to be treasured more than anything else in the world." – **Trey Parker and Matt Stone**

When people are asked in surveys what gives meaning to their lives, friendships always comes out top of the list. We usually become friendly with those who cross our paths frequently – neighbours, workmates, colleagues and people we meet socially in the pub, club or elsewhere. It is not surprising that we form bonds with those we frequently interact with and with people that we have something in common. People like those who display loyalty, trust and acceptance. So develop a more trusting approach to others. We are in fact biologically predisposed to trust others as thousands of years ago we organised ourselves into close knit groups for protection and survival.

Tips for Good Conversation

To start a conversation, say something connected to the social situation or about topical current affairs issues. This shows your willingness to talk. During the conversation make comments that are connected to what is said. You don't have to be funny or clever; all you have to be is pleasant. Use open-ended questions to keep a conversation going or elaborate on what someone else has already said. Realise that the body language should support the verbal message, otherwise contradictory signals will be given. Good conversationalists are sensitive to the signals given off by other people's body language as to whether or not they find the topic interesting. Once the conversation gets going back off and give others a chance to say their piece. Social bores dominate a conversation while socially competent people want to help others have a better conversation.

> *"A conversation is a dialogue, not a monologue. That's why there are few good conversations: due to scarcity, two intelligent talkers seldom meet."* –
> **Truman Capote**

To help conversations flow, apply the two rules of brainstorming. Say things without trying to impress people, and don't judge ideas as they come up. Others will feel more relaxed and get more freely involved in the conversation if they don't think what they say will be judged and criticised. Realise that there are different perspectives to every issue. Don't take things personally and be quick to forgive and forget when people make remarks that are unintentionally hurtful. People have their own little idiosyncrasies that you must overlook and accommodate. Listen with empathy and seek feedback.

> *"There is no such thing as a worthless conversation,*
> *provided you know what to listen for. And questions*
> *are the breath of life for a conversation."* – James
> **Nathan Miller**

SOME DIFFERENCES BETWEEN MEN
AND WOMEN

Differences between the sexes are noticed from childhood. Boys strive for independence from their mother while girls value interdependence and define their identity through their social connections. Boys' play often involves competitive group activities while girls' play happens in smaller groups, with less aggression, more sharing and more intimate discussion. Women spend more time caring for both young children and aged parents. They buy most birthday gifts and greeting cards. They outnumber men in most of the caring professions such as nursing, social work and teaching. The burden of looking after frail and elderly parents often falls on the daughters.

Men and women have different communication styles as well. Women tend to be more verbal using twice as many words as men. In contrast, men are more non-verbal, often preferring action to talking. Generally, men are programmed not to talk about or express their emotional needs. Men prefer to concentrate on physical things like hobbies, travel, cars, sports, work and politics. Women are more expressive; men tend to conceal or control their emotions.

> *"A man's brain has a more difficult time shifting from*
> *thinking to feeling than a women's brain has."* – **Bar-**
> **bara De Angelis**

Men often complain about their wives' volatility and this has some truth. Research confirms that women really are both happier and sadder than men. Women are perceived as having more empathy than men. Women experience more of all emotions except anger. They experience more positive emotions than men, more frequently and more intensely. Women convey emotion through facial expression and communication; men express emotion through aggressive behaviour. When sad, women are more prone to shed tears and express emotion than men.

Men are more likely to confide in women than other men when they are looking for empathy and understanding. However, women are more likely to confide in other women when disclosing their joys and hurts. Male friendships tend to be less supportive and intimate than women's, and they rarely share feelings or personal reflections. Women's ability to make more intimate and lasting ties with other people may account for their longevity as on average they live six to seven years longer than men.

On the other hand, women like to gossip, share personal information and are eager to talk about emotional issues and their concerns and feelings. With women now considered the equal of men in all areas of professional, occupational, social and political life, there is more scope for cross-sex friendships without the sexual connotations. In previous generations it was taboo to have friendships with the opposite sex outside of marriage. In the modern world there are more opportunities for men and women to meet at work and socially than ever before.

Surveys show that women are more satisfied at work than men, in spite of earning less for the same jobs and doing most of the work at home too. The reason for this seems to be that women's expectations of working life are lower than men's. Psychologically, men still consider themselves to be the breadwinners even though this notion is probably outmoded with both partners working in most households and in some cases women earning more than men. Women also occupy a variety of roles. A man out of work is seen as unemployed whereas a woman with a child who is out of work is seen as a full-time mother.

The area joining the left side and the right side of the brain is called the corpus callosum. The corpus callosum is thicker in women than in men. This means it is easier for messages to pass from the left side to the right side of the brain. This may facilitate the supposed superiority of women in multitasking enabling them to think and do more than one thing at a time.

"When women are depressed they either eat or go shopping. Men invade another country."– Elayne Booster

---

SUMMARY

Without sound relationships there is little scope for happiness. Develop the skill of unconditional love by loving people for who they really are without continually finding fault by highlighting their personal shortcomings. Unconditional love allows us to love and be loved. Nurture your friendships with tender loving care if you want to keep them for a lifetime.

Accept and appreciate your partner's love. Touch is the language of love including sex, caresses and cuddles. Relationships are nurtured by love, kind words and displays of affection. Married couples are happier than single people and cohabiting couples. The sense of security and permanence that marriage offers seems to make the difference. The least happy people are those trapped in unhappy marriages. Divorced, separated and widowed people may be unhappy for many years after the event and may never completely revert to their former levels of happiness.

Empathy is an important part of good relationships. Empathy can be emotional or rational. To practise empathy you must understand that people see things differently. Trust is very important to friendship. When trust is broken in a marriage or friendship the relationship cannot be sustained. Men and women have different communication styles. Men generally are programmed not to talk about their emotional needs while women are the opposite.

Five Activities to Improve Your Happiness

1) Take a genuine interest in what your friend does. Keep in touch with your friends by going out with them occasionally and by emailing and phoning them frequently.

2) Don't undermine your partner's self-esteem by criticising or belittling them in front of others. Instead take every opportunity to boost their self-esteem and show them appreciation for the friendship, support, love and happiness they bring into your life.

3) Anticipate and meet your partner's wants, needs and interests. They will appreciate your efforts.

4) Display emotional empathy to your partner by sincerely feeling their pain and expressing your concern. Never show contempt as it may lead to an irretrievable breakdown of relationships.

5) Show unconditional love to your partner and make them feel wanted, secure and safe in the relationship.

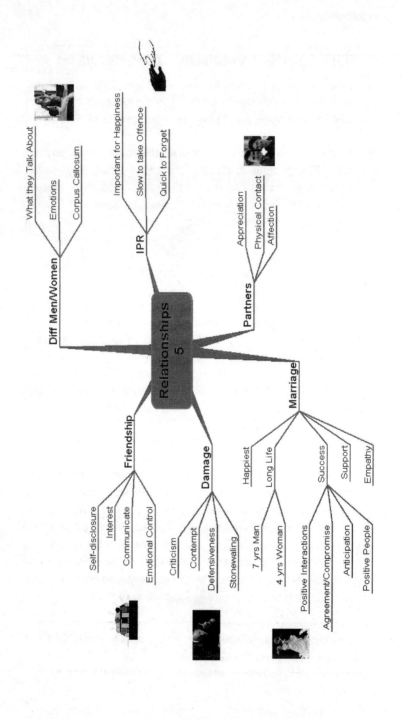

Relationships 5

Diff Men/Women
- What they Talk About
- Emotions
- Corpus Callosum

IPR
- Important for Happiness
- Slow to take Offence
- Quick to Forget

Partners
- Appreciation
- Physical Contact
- Affection

Friendship
- Self-disclosure
- Interest
- Communicate
- Emotional Control

Damage
- Criticism
- Contempt
- Defensiveness
- Stonewaling

Marriage
- Happiest
- Long Life
  - 7 yrs Man
  - 4 yrs Woman
- Success
  - Positive Interactions
  - Agreement/Compromise
  - Anticipation
  - Positive People
- Support
- Empathy

6

WORK AND HAPPINESS

❖ *What are the three ways you can view work?*

❖ *What are the four approaches to cooperation at work?*

❖ *How do toxic workers behave?*

❖ *What are the ways you can be happier at work?*

INTRODUCTION

There are three ways in which you can view work: as a job, as a career or as a calling. A calling creates the greatest degree of happiness in work as people find it intrinsically rewarding. Surveys show that workers in the USA work longer hours than anywhere else. Having balance in your life is a vital part of emotional and mental well-being. Surveys show that hairdressers and beauticians are the happiest people at work. There are many ways to be happier at work including doing work that you enjoy and treating co-workers with courtesy, consideration and respect. Toxic workers create unhappy workplaces.

"Employment is nature's physician, and is essential to human happiness." – **Galen**

PERCEPTION OF WORK

Standard economic theory assumes that time spent in leisure gives us pleasure while time spent in work gives us pain. This suggests that we only work because we have to – we need money to survive and pay our way. In different circumstances, we would prefer leisure to work. However, in reality most people like their jobs, and would work even if they didn't have to. This is confirmed by people who inherit wealth or win significant amounts of money in the lotto and return to their work shortly afterwards. Some experts maintain that after the family, work is the second most important factor affecting people's happiness.

Bertrand Russell, the British philosopher, argued that work was essential to happiness. To Russell, even the dullest of work is better than being idle. Work occupies many hours of the day for employees; it provides a chance for success and an opportunity to socialise. Work allows the exercise and development of skill and provides a sense of achievement when the job is completed. If people perceive themselves and their work is of a high value they will be motivated. Productivity, commitment and cooperation also increase when people hold a positive perception about their work.

"Happiness is made up of three factors: positive emotion; being completely engaged; and feeling you are part of something meaningful. If you have engagement, energy and meaning at work, it leads to higher productivity." – Martin Seligman

There are three ways in which you can view work: as a job, as a career or as a calling. The perception you have of work will determine the amount of job satisfaction that you will enjoy and the amount of happiness you will derive from the experience. People with prestigious jobs like lawyers and architects are often unhappy, while those with seemingly low level jobs such as hairdressing and beauticians are often very contented. Some experts have estimated that lawyers are 3.6 times more likely to be depressed than members of other professions, and think this is because of the adversarial nature of their work. Work plays a central part to most of our lives, gives us a sense of identity and takes up the most significant part of our time. So it's important that we enjoy what we do.

A job is not usually seen as contributing to our long-term goals or aspirations. Many people, if they had a choice, would not be doing the work that they are currently doing. They focus on the financial and social rewards rather than any personal fulfilment the job offers. They look forward to the end of each work day and regard their hobbies and leisure time as more important than their work.

People with a career, on the other hand, often enjoy their work. Money is a factor, though the status and possibilities for advancement and job satisfaction are often considered more important. Some research has suggested that our perception of our social standing, which is linked to our occupation within our local communities, determines our sense of well-being. People with a career are usually professionally qualified and loyalty to the profession is often stronger than loyalty to a particular employer. Because their profession can be practised in different organisations their skills are transferable. They are thus very mobile and may seek out companies offering them the best prospects for advancement. They place a high value on leisure activities and think a lot about their holidays.

"Not only does happiness feel good, but happy people appear to function better than unhappy people – making more money, having better social relationships, being better organisational citizens at work, doing more volunteer work and having better health." – **Ed Diener**

People with a calling are paid to do work they would love to do anyway. Professions like teaching, the church and nursing attract people with a calling. Any type of job can be turned into a calling depending on the attitude of the job holder. All you need is scope to personalise and make the job better. People who really enjoy their work feel it isn't work. They work hard because they find the work intrinsically rewarding and feel that they are making a significant contribution to society. They see the work as an end in itself and are likely to stay with the company longer.

"If you plan on being anything less than you are capable of being, you will probably be unhappy all the days of your life." – **Abraham Maslow**

WORK–LIFE BALANCE

Surveys show that workers in the USA work longer hours than those in Europe. GDP per head is higher but productivity is the same. Happiness has stood still in the US since 1975 while it has risen in Europe. In addition, employers are putting more emphasis on efficiency, productivity, achieving targets, quality and cost effectiveness and so there is more pressure on workers. There are more rules and less trust so that people feel they have no discretion and less control over their work. All work and no play will make Jack a dull boy and it is likely to make him a sick boy too. So it's important that people spend sufficient time in recreational activities away from the pressures of work.

Having balance in your life is a vital part of emotional and mental well-being. If you're dissatisfied with the quality of your life, take some time to reflect on your physical, emotional and spiritual needs. Flexible working may be suitable for some people in terms of where and when they work and the sense of control over their lives that they get back. Flexible working arrangements include part-time work, job sharing, term-time hours, annualised hours, childcare facilities onsite, unpaid leave and an increase in working from home. When people are free to work at times suited to them they will be happier and more productive overall.

Employers should respect employee needs to balance work and home life. Research in ten European countries in 2006 suggests that we get more satisfaction from activities outside of work. The most common examples would be a sport, which provides plenty of challenges, and also creative leisure activities such as art, amateur dramatics and chess. In fact, anything that demands a level of skill, unlike watching television which is purely a passive and a mind-numbing activity. In another study, volunteering came second, after dancing, as the greatest source of joy. Research also shows that making trade-offs for promotion or a higher salary, such as accepting a longer commute to work or sacrificing time with family and friends, is rarely worth it. You may enjoy the new status, power and higher salary but feel stressed by the longer hours and extra responsibility and the changed attitudes of your former work colleagues.

"Those who are caught up in the busy life have neither the time nor quiet to come to understand themselves and their goals. Since the opportunity for inward attention hardly ever comes, many people have not heard from themselves for a long time. Those who are always 'on the run' never meet anybody any more, not even themselves." – **Robert Banks**

Stress at Work

Stress causes heart disease and premature death. So working long hours is bad for your health and will wreck relationships. In addition, tired employees are irritable with co-workers and customers and so bad for business. An excessive workload may cause stress which may in turn lead to burnout and sick leave for the employee. (The topic of stress is dealt with more comprehensively in Chapter 14.)

Burnout is a state of physical, emotional and mental exhaustion caused by prolonged involvement in work that is too intellectually and emotionally demanding. People suffering from burnout may be anxious, agitated, apathetic, bored and confused. They may abuse alcohol or drugs and be distressed at times. They often suffer from sleep deprivation because they are so irritable after work that they are unable to unwind and so become so exhausted and fatigued that they can't sleep. People who are burned out have two to three times the risk of heart problems, including recurrent myocardial infarction, stroke, coronary-bypass surgery, atherosclerosis and cardiac arrest. Burnout results in unhappiness for the individual and may cause substantial costs for an organisation due to higher staff turnover, absenteeism and reduced productivity. To counteract feelings of burnout, take frequent breaks, relax and get involved in work activities that create flow.

Work–Life Surveys

In surveys, hairdressers, beauticians, plumbers and chefs say they are happy at work. In contrast, some of the best paid jobs and professions like civil servants, estate agents, architects, bankers, accountants, pharmacists, media personnel and lawyers say that they are unhappy. Generally, the people who rank high on general happiness are those who work in professions involving helping others, using technical and scientific expertise or involving creativity. The jobs with the least happy people are ones that are high pressured or else routine and unskilled manual and service positions.

Surveys show that, despite leading a glamorous life, models are often unhappy. The factors affecting happiness are said to be loving relationships and feelings of being competent and in control. Models surveyed lacked all three. Models are explicitly valued for superficial reasons such as their appearance and not for their intrinsic personal qualities such as personality, wit and talent. The working lifetime of a model is also short as beauty fades and thus there is a lot of insecurity in the profession as a continuous supply of younger and more beautiful models become available. The study concluded that despite their beauty, models were no happier than anyone else and considerably less satisfied.

"There is only one boss – the customer. And he can fire everybody in the company from the chairman on down, simply by spending his money somewhere else."
– Sam Walton

It seems it pays to be happy at your job. People who are happy in their work are healthier. A study by a team from University College London tested the happiness levels of 216 middle-aged civil servants for coronary disease risk factors. They found that people who had the happiest moments per day had the lowest rates of cortisol, a hormone that can be harmful to the heart if produced excessively. On the other hand, the Whitehall Study shows that people with low status jobs with little say and control over what they do have a higher risk of cardiovascular disease. Since the 1960s, Professor Sir Michael Marmot and colleagues at University College London have been studying thousands of civil servants for an ongoing research project. Their findings are contrary to the conventional wisdom where you would expect lower level jobs to be less stressful and therefore more congenial to health.

Happy people are less likely to lose their jobs and, if they do, more likely to be re-employed quickly. According to research published in 2008 by City and Guilds, beauticians are the happiest workers in the UK, followed by hairdressers, chefs and soldiers. People who work with their hands tend to be far happier at work than those who don't, particularly when their jobs combine an intellectual challenge with practical skills and immediate feedback. Journalists are more than midway down the list of job satisfaction, while right at the bottom are bankers and other financial services workers. Beauticians and hairdressers make people feel happier about themselves and they get to interact with their customers in a most satisfying way. Some women even maintain that visits to the hairdresser and gossiping with their friends are among the things that make them happiest.

The discipline of army life, the sense of doing your patriotic duty and the camaraderie involved probably is the source of job satisfaction for soldiers. Catering, including chefs and retail staff, also figured high on the happiness index. Chefs see themselves as culinary artists and some even achieve celebrity status. Journalists, mechanics, HR managers, call centre staff, IT specialists and nurses did badly as regards happiness at work. The survey findings for nurses are surprising as they are in a helping profession. On the other hand, it is not surprising that bankers and accountants came out badly as they get very bad press and people's trust in them is very low. The Enron collapse in 2001 and the global banking crisis in 2008–09 will have worsened the situation. Bankers in particular are reviled for their greed and reckless lending to secure bonuses.

"Friendly co-workers, along with good managers and a desirable commute, topped the list of items that create overall workplace happiness." – Salary.com's 2005/2006 Employee Satisfaction and Retention Survey

---

CREATING HAPPY WORKERS

In their quest for personal excellence people are influenced by the expectations of others and by their own high expectations. People respond according to the way they are treated. The Pygmalion Effect suggests that in addition to our own expectations we live up to the expectations of others. In experiments, students were found to live up to the high expectations set by their teachers. If they were treated with respect and as being clever they did better in their examinations. Similarly, if our managers set high standards we are often motivated to achieve them even if we are pushed beyond our comfort zone, provided we are treated with dignity and respect. Managers can draw out the best in people by leading by example, treating them as intelligent, resourceful, creative and empowered human beings. On the other hand, they can draw out the worst in people by setting a bad example, by having low expectations and by treating them as lacking in intelligence, ideas and initiative. Gandhi said that you should be the change you want to see in the world. It is not logical for senior managers to expect employees to accept pay cuts when they earn more in a year than employees earn in a lifetime.

"The difference between a lady and a flower girl is not how she behaves but how she's treated. I shall always be a flower girl to Professor Higgins because he always treats me as a flower girl." – **Eliza Dolittle, in George Bernard Shaw's play** *Pygmalion*

The Manager's Role in Happiness

It is a manager's job to create a listening culture and to be accessible when employees need them. Managers should spend more time in exploring individual needs, listening to people's likes and dislikes and career aspirations. If they did this they would win over employee commitment and engagement. When managers create a two-way dialogue they find out what is going on in the company, what problems employees are experiencing, the potential problems on the horizon and what they can do to resolve the situation. If they do this they will increase performance, productivity and profitability.

When managers compliment employees that their performance meets or exceeds desired standards it enhances motivation through the positive feelings and pride generated by the feedback. Managers sometimes forget that the easiest and cheapest way of lifting the spirit of demotivated workers is to tell them they are doing a good job. Employees like managers to listen to their concerns, accommodate their needs and appreciate and recognise their efforts. In practice, effective communication is a problem in most companies and not enough time and money is invested to rectify the problem. People are often promoted into management positions without the necessary communication and interpersonal relationship skills.

"Never continue in a job you don't enjoy. If you're happy in what you're doing, you'll like yourself, you'll have inner peace. And if you have that, along with physical health, you will have had more success than you could possibly have imagined." – Johnny Carson

---

People prefer jobs offering prestige and standing in the community. They like to feel that their talents are being used and that their contribution to the company is valued. They like jobs with clear expectations and directions on how to meet them and with feedback on how they are doing. Clear expectations should be set out in job descriptions and the policies and procedures of the company will tell you about the company's history, operations, hours of operation and standard operating procedures.

Happy Workers Are Busy

People are happier when they are productive rather than underemployed. One survey found that people who think their work allows them to be productive are about five times more likely to be very satisfied with their jobs than people who do not feel they can be productive. Help people be productive by fostering a culture of continuous improvement, lifelong learning, training and development, getting the workforce involved in business issues and empowering employees to find their own solutions to problems. People who are dissatisfied with their jobs are about seven times more likely to quit within a year than those who are very satisfied.

Everybody in the company should be encouraged to be creative and to use their initiative. Creativity leads to innovation and provides a company with a competitive edge as intellectual capital is becoming the principal asset of many companies. People can often spot potential areas for improvement on the shop floor and with outdated processes and procedures. Creativity within a company should not be confined to marketing and research and development, but instead should be encouraged and rewarded throughout the company.

In the modern workplace the opposite is happening with a trend towards more management control over workers and lack of job security which makes for an unhappy workforce. This is evidenced by the setting of more demanding targets, incentive-based payments, performance appraisal, performance-related pay, constantly changing work practices and increased monitoring and surveillance by first line managers and supervisors. This has been matched by a culture of long hours and contractual and financial insecurity, even for middle class professionals. This has put workers under additional pressure – workers who are already crippled by debt and high mortgage repayments and living in constant fear that they will lose their jobs.

> *"I am suggesting to you the simple idea that people work harder and smarter if they find their work satisfying and know that it is appreciated."* – **Robert F. Six**

Pay and Security

People are happy as long as the pay they receive is the same or greater than those they work with. They are less concerned about what people earn in other organisations. This means making sure that people are recognised and rewarded appropriately for the effort they put in and for their unique talents. Pay rivalry within organisations is a well known fact, however, which is why organisations try to maintain peace in the workplace by keeping people's wages secret. The more your coworker earns relative to you the more dissatisfied you will become. You are more concerned about the relative income rather than its absolute value. Over the years the pay and opportunities for women has improved considerably relative to men, but their level of happiness has not. This is because they compare themselves more specifically to men than they used to, and are therefore more aware of the gaps that still exist relative to the pay of men for similar work.

People who have secure jobs are happier as they are confident of a regular cash flow to meet everyday living expenses and mortgage repayments. One survey showed that people who say their job security is bad are six times more likely to be dissatisfied with their jobs than those who say their security is good. Japanese employers realise this and are extremely reluctant to make their workers redundant even in recessionary times. There is a strong case for retaining a skilled workforce in an economic downturn because it is very time-consuming and expensive to train people when the economy picks up again.

Boeing, once the largest single source of exports in the US, cut its workforce by more than one-third and production by more than 40 per cent in 1993 in response to a cyclical downturn in the aircraft industry. A protest strike by their employees only increased costs and losses. Three years later, when orders began to increase again, Boeing found it had too few experienced managers and skilled workers to take advantage of the economic upswing.

"Management by objective works – if you know the objective. Ninety per cent of the time you don't." – **Peter Drucker**

Toxic Workers

Toxic workers create unhappy workplaces. They love to be disruptive and take a delight in upsetting others. They engage in office politics, image building, game playing, manipulation, bullying and harassment. They treat their work colleagues as pawns rather than partners. They are negative people and never agree to anything. They never see the merits in any proposal and are opposed to any change in the workplace. They are stress carriers – creating stress for those they come in contact without creating stress for themselves. They tend to be aggressive, use obscenities and be sarcastic and opinionated. They can make you ill with anxiety, depression and stress as likely outcomes. A toxic workplace with high pressure deadlines can increase the risk of health problems for workers.

WAYS TO BE HAPPIER AT WORK

- Treat co-workers with courtesy, consideration and respect and they in turn will treat you likewise. People in a happy workplace feel they have been included within the business vision and have a strong sense of belonging. When morale is high, energy levels will be high and people will be less prone to illness and taking days off.

- Live close to the workplace. People who commute long distances to and from work are unhappy. Commuting in heavy traffic is stressful and not conducive to a sense of well-being. It is also a waste of valuable time that you could productively use elsewhere such as spending more time with your family. Sometimes it's a question of making a trade-off between a larger and a smaller house closer to work in order to reduce commute time.

- Work for a small company where you can readily see the contribution you make to the objectives of the organisation. In a large company, because of specialisation and scale, it can be difficult to see exactly how you fit in to the overall scheme of things. Small companies also facilitate more intimate and less formal relationships with other employees and management.

- Find an organisation where you feel a sense of connection and belonging. Reflect on what you expect from work and what truly motivates you. Ask yourself the following searching questions: Does your work make you feel satisfied and appreciated? Do you feel committed and proud of your job? Would you like to be doing what you're doing in five years' time?

- Work in a company whose objectives and way of doing business are in harmony with your beliefs and values. You will never be happy in a company where you feel uncomfortable with the way it conducts its business and treats its employees and customers.

- Work in a job that uses your unique skills. You want a job that is meaningful and makes a contribution to the world. As Franklin D. Roosevelt observed, happiness lies in the joy of achievement and in the thrill of creative effort.

- If you feel a negative spiral coming on, counteract it with positive self-talk. When you are in a positive mood, you are more creative, more motivated to perform better, more energetic and more helpful towards colleagues.

- Turn a stalled career into a calling by thinking about the elements of the job that you like and the contribution you are making to society. Otherwise, explore opportunities for different job placements within the company or projects that might bring fresh experiences, challenges and stimulation.

- Take a career break when you find that the job is not offering the satisfaction it once did. Taking a break to do something that you really want to do will give you the zest that you need when returning to your job.

- Downshift if you think you are working too hard and need more time for family, friends, other interests or recreational pursuits.

- Although the risks are high, most people find that working for themselves provides the greatest source of satisfaction as you have more control over how you spend your time.

- Break your job down into parts that you enjoy and parts that you don't enjoy. Do the parts that you don't like first. The expectation of enjoyable work will keep you going.

- Act as if you enjoy what you do even if you don't and eventually it will become a self-fulfilling prophecy. You must love what you do if you want to be consistently successful and happy.

"In order that people may be happy in their work, these three things are needed: They must be fit for it. They must not do too much of it. And they must have a sense of success in it." – **John Ruskin**

SUMMARY

Work plays a central role in most of our lives and takes up a significant part of our time. So it's important that we are happy at work. Treat your job as a calling to maximise your level of happiness. People in the USA work longer hours than elsewhere and are less happy. Stress and burnout are features of work in a modern developed economy. Pressures to meet tight deadlines can cause anxiety and undue stress.

Work–life surveys show that some jobs bring more happiness than others. Happy workers find job satisfaction in what they do. Toxic workers create unhappy workplaces. Their behaviour tends to be destructive rather than constructive. You are more likely to be happy at work if you live close to your workplace, work in a job that uses your unique strengths and enjoy what you do.

Five Activities to Improve Your Happiness

1) Even if there is a lot of routine in your job challenge yourself by seeing how various tasks and methods could be improved. There are always different ways of doing anything – some more efficient than others. Constant improvement should be your aim.

2) Treat your co-workers with courtesy, consideration and respect. They are likely to do likewise so that everybody benefits especially customers.

3) Help others at work if they need your assistance. Become known as someone who is willing to help if called on to do so.

4) Take a career break if you find you are going stale on the job. This will re-invigorate your attitude when you return to the job.

5) Downshift if you are spending too much time at work. This will give you more time to spend with family and friends and pursue recreational interests that you are keen on.

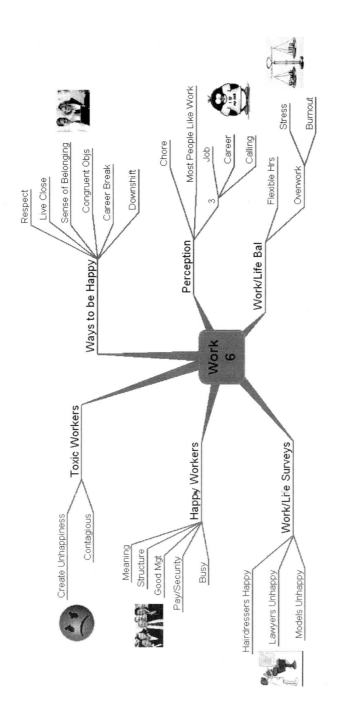

Work 6

Ways to be Happy
- Respect
- Live Close
- Sense of Belonging
- Congruent Objs
- Career Break
- Downshift

Perception
- Chore
- Most People Like Work
- 3
  - Job
  - Career
  - Calling

Work/Life Bal
- Flexible Hrs
- Overwork
  - Stress
  - Burnout

Toxic Workers
- Create Unhappiness
- Contagious

Happy Workers
- Meaning
- Structure
- Good Mgt
- Pay/Security
- Busy

Work/Life Surveys
- Hairdressers Happy
- Lawyers Unhappy
- Models Unhappy

7

HAPPINESS AT HOME

- ❖ *What are the characteristics of happy families?*
- ❖ *What are the four parenting styles?*
- ❖ *Which style is considered the best?*
- ❖ *How can you develop a happy relationship with your family?*
- ❖ *Do children always make you happy?*

INTRODUCTION

Most parents don't realise that there are different parenting styles, some of which are more successful than others. The authoritative parenting style is a high discipline and high participative style. Children operate within clear boundaries and so have a clear idea of their role and the expectations of their parents. The style fosters independence, initiative and self-control.

Parents should teach their children that life is not plain sailing and that happiness is something to strive for rather than an entitlement. Allow children to fail and learn from their mistakes to teach them resilience. Teach them that life is meaningful, to have belief in themselves, good values, seek help from others when they need to, set personal goals and recognise their strengths to achieve them.

Intuitively you would say that children make parents happy but the research is mixed and often seems to suggest otherwise. Like anything else in life, having children has its highs and lows and its joys and frustrations. Though challenging and burdensome, many people find parenthood a meaningful role providing a sense of purpose to life. However, even with the best of parenting skills some children turn out bad and become a source of torment and worry to their parents. In reality, couples can be happy with or without children. Some couples sacrifice children to concentrate on their careers and lead happy and meaningful lives without the burden of children.

"Feelings of worth can flourish only in an atmosphere where individual differences are appreciated, mistakes are tolerated, communication is open, and rules are flexible – the kind of atmosphere that is found in a nurturing family." – **Virginia Satir**

Happy Families

Good family relationships provide our greatest comfort and joy. In contrast, dysfunctional family relationships can be a source of great heartaches and stress. Happy families respect individual differences and treat each other equally. They have unconditional love for each other, are prepared to make sacrifices to help each other and are prepared to overlook personal shortcomings. They are interdependent and cooperate to their mutual advantage. They share common values, goals and have a clearly defined purpose and sense of direction. They share common activities and recreational pastimes. They support each other and help each other to overcome difficult situations. In times of crises they unite and present a common front. They have a clear sense of identity and a clear sense of values. They know their family history and realise that the family is a link to the past and a bridge to the future. They have a sense of stability and pride in their roots and traditions. They plan for the future as best they can while being mindful of the present.

> **"Perhaps the greatest social service that can be rendered by anybody to this country and to mankind is to bring up a family." – George Bernard Shaw**

Happy families handle anger constructively. They don't treat each other with contempt but instead allow for and try to accommodate individual differences. Contempt undermines family relationships and self-esteem and should be relentlessly discouraged by parents. Siblings should be taught to respect each other. Parents should begin with their own relationship and never show contempt to their partner. Example is what children learn best from rather than empty words. Good parents show emotional constraint and practise discipline in a non-physical manner. Conflicts are solved in non-competitive ways using accommodating or collaborative strategies.

Happy families share power but do so in sensible and equitable ways. Children are given responsibility for certain tasks appropriate to their age and stage of development. This encourages them from an early age to become self-sufficient and responsible citizens. Parents praise their children for improved or exceptional performance. They know that praise should be genuine and earned as otherwise it loses its impact and value.

Happy families know the art of compromise and try to avoid futile arguments. Members treat each other with courtesy and respect. Small issues are not allowed to fester and be blown out of proportion. Instead, they are solved before they become major issues. They acknowledge and respect each other's need for privacy and space.

PARENTING STYLES

The influence parents have on their children is very strong. Early relationships with the child play a critical role in character formation, in the growth of personality and the development of attitudes towards other people. Attitudes and behaviours we learned in the family growing up are repeated unconsciously throughout our lives. Most parents don't realise that there are different styles of parenting, some of which are more successful than others. We are trained for many roles in life but few of us get any training in the art of parenting – the most demanding role in life. We want our children to grow up into principled adults who are moral, truthful, honest and ethical. This is not an easy task in a world where there are so few role models left as many of our leaders in business, politics and the church have been found to be seriously flawed. Children are a precious gift and a challenge to rear but few of us give it the thought, time and attention that it deserves. People get married and become parents without any preparation and training whatsoever.

"Having children makes you no more a parent than having a piano makes you a pianist." – **Michael Levine**

There are four parenting styles: autocratic, authoritative, permissive and unengaged. The following is a model of the various styles:

	PARTICIPATION	
	High	Low
DISCIPLINE High	Authoritative	Autocratic
DISCIPLINE Low	Permissive	Unengaged

1. **Autocratic.** This is a high discipline and low participative style of parenting. The autocratic style is a command and control approach to parenting. The parents decide every-

thing and the child has no say. The parents decide what the child does, where the child goes and the type of friends the child has. The parents hope to control ultimately what the child's life will be. This style fosters dependence. Autocratic parents tend to criticise a lot and be cold and emotionally aloof. In such an environment, as children mature and assert themselves they may rebel against their parent's authority.

"Home is the place where boys and girls learn how to limit their wishes, abide by the rules, and consider the rights and needs of others." **– Sidonie Gruenberg**

---

2. **Authoritative**. This is a high discipline and a high partici-pative style of parenting. The parents exercise a reasonable amount of control with clear boundaries so that children know exactly what they can and cannot do. They trust their children to operate freely within these boundaries unless events prove otherwise. They are highly involved in the child's life and tend to be firm but fair. Discipline is non-physical with an emphasis on withdrawal of rights and privileges. These are restored when behaviour improves. Authoritative parents offer their children lots of support, unconditional love and acceptance. Children have a clear idea of their role and the expectations of their parents. The style fosters independence, initiative and self-control.

3. **Permissive**. This is a low discipline and a high participative style of parenting. It is a lax style where parents leave their children do as they please. The children may have no re-spect for the property of others. The parents have a hands-off approach and tend to shy away from conflict. The at-mosphere in the home can be warm and loving. The style may foster lack of discipline and self-control in children and is likely to be a poor preparation for the realities of life such as the discipline required to work effectively and op-erate within a regulatory work environment.

4. **Unengaged.** This low participative and low discipline style is a laissez faire approach to parenting. Unengaged parents have no philosophy of how to rear children and so let them rear themselves. The parents are uninvolved, unconcerned and unaware of what their children are up to. They are allowed to play on the streets without any supervision. The children are given little direction and little emotional support. Such children will be more influenced by their peers than their parents. They have no clear expectations for their children who operate without clear boundaries as to what they can and cannot do.

"I have found the best way to give advice to your children is to find out what they want and then advise them to do it." – Harry S. Truman

---

THE AUTHORITATIVE DIFFERENCE

The ideal parenting style is a balance of interdependence with autonomy. Some parents are overprotective and find it difficult to give their children a reasonable amount of freedom. Your aim as a parent is to rear children to become well adjusted, confident and self-reliant adults who are happy in their own skin and make their own way in life as independent and responsible citizens. As a parent you should ensure that everyone has a role or a job to do within the family household. This gives children a sense of purpose and responsibility. Children should be encouraged to collaborate and swap roles when that suits them.

Certain things can be done collectively, such as doing housework. Children should also help around the house generally and in the garden. Tasks should be matched with their strengths and preferences. The child with a love of animals should be given the task of looking after the family pet. Children should be encouraged to help each other, especially during times of illness. Parents should help with homework and encourage the older children to assist the younger ones. The family should engage in recreational pursuits together. As children grow up and leave the home, reunions such as Christmas, Easter and birthdays are important to maintain a sense of togetherness and solidarity.

The authoritative style of parenting helps give the family a sense of connectedness. It helps the children to grow up to be socially and emotionally competent adults. In such an environment the child grows up feeling secure and free from a sense of anxiety. They are more likely to be confident, independent, resilient and determined when pursuing their goals. Parents should guide and encourage their child to set goals that are challenging but realistic having regard to the child's unique strengths and weaknesses. Children are more likely to pursue goals that they had a part in making. The low expectations of parents may become a self-fulfilling prophecy if the goals set are too easy to achieve. The self-esteem of children will go up when they accomplish reasonably difficult tasks. This would act as an encouragement to undertake more challenging tasks.

Authoritative parents are slow to criticise but when they do they criticise the behaviour of the child rather than the child itself. They love the child unconditionally but not the mischievous behaviour. They try to criticise the behaviour in a constructive way so as not to undermine the child's confidence and sense of self-esteem. Parents should encourage their children to take an interest in current affairs and in the world around them and in people generally. They should teach them to respect other people, especially the elderly, and treat everyone with courtesy and consideration.

> *"Parents can only give good advice or put them on the right paths, but the final forming of a person's character lies in their own hands."* **– Anne Frank**

DEVELOPING HAPPY FAMILY RELATIONSHIPS

The family meal is a great time to build solidarity and meaningful social ties within the family. Families should aim to have at least one meal per day together. Never let the family meal deteriorate into a battlefield between siblings. Children should be allowed to ventilate rather than vent their feelings. Ventilation is rational discussion while venting is the emotional expression of anger. The family meal should be used as an opportunity to catch up on news, discuss current affairs, review the activities and achievements of the day and to plan future events. Getting your point of view across and debating skills can be nurtured at the family table. Take every opportunity to genuinely praise your child in proportion to the success achieved. If parents are too ready to praise it loses its value.

Parents should treat their children like friends with respect, courtesy and interest. Treat them equally and avoid favouritism. They should teach their children that life is full of ups and downs and that happiness is something to strive for and not an entitlement. Allow children to fail and learn from their mistakes. Teach them a love of learning and that lifelong learning is essential for success in the modern world. Teach them resilience by encouraging them to bounce back when they encounter failures and setbacks. After all, real life is full of disappointments, difficulties, loss and inconveniences. Encourage them to dust themselves off and start all over again. If they have a natural talent give them the necessary encouragement and support to exploit it to the full.

> *"To nourish children and raise them against odds is in any time, any place, more valuable than to fix bolts in cars or design nuclear weapons."* – Marilyn French

Limit television viewing and supervise internet activity. Encourage your children to read and use the internet as a resource for research and information. Discourage materialism in your children as highly materialistic people are less happy than those with more balanced priorities. Family relationships and recreational pursuits are more important than material possessions. Sulking is a type of emotional blackmail and so the sulking child should not be given into. Children should be taught to share sweets and toys with others, have fun activities and share holidays together. It is more important to spend time with your children rather than lavish them with expensive presents and generous pocket money allowances.

Do Children Make You Happy?

Intuitively, you would say yes but the research is mixed and often seems to suggest otherwise. For example, in Daniel Gilbert's 2006 book *Stumbling on Happiness*, the Harvard professor of psychology looks at several studies and concludes that marital satisfaction decreases dramatically after the birth of the first child and increases only when the last child has left home. He also claims that parents are happier when shopping for their groceries, watching television and sleeping than being with their children. Other studies show that women are more likely to claim that children make them happier.

"Cultural expectations shade and colour the images that parents-to-be form. The baby product ads, showing a woman serenely holding her child, looking blissfully and mysteriously contented, or the television parents, wisely and humorously solving problems, influence parents-to-be." – **Ellen Galinsky**

There is great joy when a child is born but after about two years people revert to their original level of happiness. The proud parents enjoy a sense of euphoria about the new arrival who they feel add meaning to their lives and will change things for the better. However, adaptation means this feeling will not last and couples get progressively less satisfied over time until their children grow up and leave home. In popular culture the "empty nest syndrome" should be renamed the "smiling nest syndrome". These findings go against the conventional wisdom, which suggests that children are the key to happiness. Advertisements suggest that parenthood is one blissful moment after another and we are disappointed when we find out that it's not.

In the pre-industrial world, children served a purpose and had an economic use. They were needed to work on the farm and contribute to the household budget. In Victorian times children were barely tolerated and were encouraged to be seen but not heard. Family pets were often more valued than children. Today, with both parents often out working, rearing children has become more complicated and more expensive. The support of the extended family and the sense of faith and community in many cases have gone and child minding costs are exorbitant. In addition, the health care and education systems are over-extended and long commutes to work don't make things any easier.

The Joys and Disappointments of Having Children

Children are very expensive to rear, tie you down and limit your social life as a couple to do the things you want to do and the things you want to achieve in life. When children are young things like going to the cinema, theatre, pub, parties and travel are postponed or enjoyed less frequently because babysitting can be difficult to organise and also expensive. If you have a handicapped child all these problems are magnified several times over. In such cases your whole life will be centred round the needs of the child, often in circumstances where you have inadequate support from the health services.

Like anything else in life, having children has its ups and downs, its highs and lows, and its joys and frustrations. Child-rearing is a full-time occupation and parents are prepared to make many sacrifices for their children's well-being. Though we are genetically programmed to look after our children, changing nappies several times a day is still an unpleasant chore. Getting up in the middle of the night to attend to a bawling baby is no fun, especially when you have to go to work the following morning tired and suffering from sleep deprivation. Rushing to a hospital in the middle of the night when your child becomes sick can also be very traumatic for the parents.

> *"Before I got married I had six theories about bringing up children; now I have six children and no theories."*
> – John Wilmot, Earl of Rochester

In the long term, raising a child is one of the most rewarding and meaningful of human experiences. Seeing your child grow up and achieve success at school or in sports can be a great source of pride. Experiencing the milestones of childhood, like their first steps and first words, brings indescribable joy to the parents. Seeing your child graduating from college and getting their first job, and later on seeing them get married and settling down, is a wonderful feeling. Furthermore, the deep love most parents have for their children is unique and hard to describe and quantify.

Indeed, children can bring great happiness, purpose and meaning and bind a couple together, or alternatively they can cause worry, anxiety, irritation, frustration, strain and conflict within the family. Even with the best of rearing, some children turn out bad and a source of torment, worry and disappointment for their parents. The more children you have the more likely it is that one or more will not live up to your expectations. Parents never stop worrying about their children, even when they grow up into adults. Modern problems like binge drinking, drug abuse, street violence, and pre-marital sex and gender identity issues only add to the worries. The increased availability of drugs and alcohol is a constant worry for parents.

Childless couples can have an unfulfilled desire and ambition for a baby that can be all consuming and lead to high levels of unhappiness. They will resort to expensive and invasive fertility treatments and artificial insemination over many years if they think this will enhance their chances of having a child. In reality, couples can be happy with or without children. Some couples sacrifice children to concentrate on their careers and lead happy and meaningful lives without the burden and worry of children.

> "One's family is the most important thing in life. I look at it this way: one of these days I'll be over in a hospital somewhere with four walls around me. And the only people who'll be with me will be my family."
> – Robert C. Byrd

SUMMARY

Happy families respect their children as individuals with unique needs and talents and treat them equally and with courtesy and consideration. There are different parenting styles, some of which are more successful than others. These styles are authoritative, autocratic, permissive and unengaged. The authoritative parenting style is recommended as the ideal style to adopt. It is a high discipline and a high participative style. Children operate within clear boundaries and so have a clear idea of their role and the expectations of their parents. The style fosters independence, initiative and self-control.

The family meal presents a great opportunity to build solidarity and meaningful social ties within the family. Families should aim to have at least one meal per day together. Never allow the family meal to deteriorate into a war between siblings. Parents should teach their children that life is full of ups and downs and that happiness is something to strive for rather than an entitlement. Allow children to fail and learn from their experience. Teach them resilience by encouraging them to bounce back when they encounter failures and setbacks.

Most people are of the opinion that children make parents happy but the research is mixed and often seems to suggest otherwise. There is great joy when a child is born but after about two years people revert to their original level of happiness. Like anything else in life having children has its ups and downs, its highs and lows, and its joys and frustrations. Even with the best of parenting skills some children turn out bad and become a source of torment and worry to their parents. In reality couples can be happy with or without children. Some couples sacrifice children to concentrate on their careers and lead happy and meaningful lives without the burden of children.

Five Activities to Improve Your Happiness at Home

1) Make sure to treat your children equally and avoid having favourites.

2) Adopt the authoritative parenting style when dealing with your children. Research suggests that this is the most successful parenting style.

3) Try to get the family together for at least one meal per day. Use the time to review the day's activities, discuss current affairs, and to enquire how your children are getting along.

4) Discourage the use of derogatory and contemptuous language between your children. Teach siblings to have respect for each other.

5) Take every opportunity to praise the achievements of your children and encourage them to develop whatever natural talents they have.

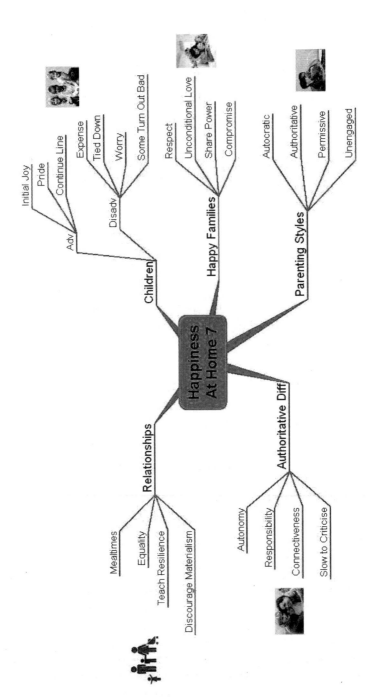

Happiness At Home 7

Children

Adv
- Initial Joy
- Pride
- Continue Line

Disadv
- Expense
- Tied Down
- Worry
- Some Turn Out Bad

Happy Families
- Respect
- Unconditional Love
- Share Power
- Compromise

Parenting Styles
- Autocratic
- Authoritative
- Permissive
- Unengaged

Relationships
- Mealtimes
- Equality
- Teach Resilience
- Discourage Materialism

Authoritative Diff
- Autonomy
- Responsibility
- Connectiveness
- Slow to Criticise

8

OPTIMISM

❖ *Why are optimists happier?*
❖ *What is realistic optimism?*
❖ *How can you counteract pessimism?*
❖ *What is the ABCDE approach?*
❖ *What is self-esteem?*

INTRODUCTION

Optimism is the tendency to believe that the best will happen. Realistic optimists have their feet on the ground and know how to deal constructively with disappointments and setbacks. Happiness is a self-fulfilling prophecy as the attitude you have today largely determines how things will turn out for you tomorrow. When you think about the past you should focus on positive events. When you think about the future you should anticipate that good things will happen to you. Right now you should focus on the present. Negative thoughts will make you unhappy, while positive thoughts will make you happy.

> *"Your living is determined not so much by what life brings to you as by the attitude you bring to life; not so much by what happens to you as by the way your mind looks at what happens." –* John Homer Miller

Use the ABCDE approach to mentally challenge negative thoughts and adverse life events. There is a difference between optimism and self-esteem. Optimism is how you view situations while self-esteem is how you evaluate yourself. Both make an important contribution to personal happiness.

"When life knocks you down, try to land on your back, because if you can look up, you can get up. Let your reason get you back up." – Les Brown

---

WHAT IS OPTIMISM?

Optimism is the tendency to believe, expect or hope that things will turn out well. There is an old saying, *your attitude determines your altitude*. In other words, a positive attitude can help you achieve great things and go far in life. Optimism, faith, self-acceptance, loyalty and industry are examples of positive attitudes. Optimists see their glass as half full rather than half empty. Optimists feel good about themselves, tend to have better moods, look for the bright side of things, see the silver lining in every cloud and focus on what's right rather than what's wrong. Because they don't turn minor setbacks into catastrophes, optimists are better able to bounce back from emotional and physical stress than others. Optimists tend to be ambitious and set themselves stretch goals. It was optimism, determination and self-belief that kept Chester Carlson, the inventor of photocopying, going when the technology he invented was rejected by more than 20 companies.

Optimism is contagious. Research has found that people enhance their own feelings of happiness by sharing positive experiences with others, who in turn become more positive and treat others more positively. Optimistic leaders in the workplace are likely to create optimistic followers. This implies that leaders can diffuse optimism into their workforce. Realistic optimists have their feet on the ground and know how to deal with disappointments and setbacks. Optimists are generally more persevering in their goals and activities because they have the confidence, commitment and motivation to overcome challenges. They are realistic about the risks involved in any decision and know when to persevere or give up and move on. Optimistic thinking can be associated with an underestimation of risks, however. For example, we do not necessarily want a pilot or air traffic controller to be an optimist when deciding whether to take off during a storm. Better to be on the safe and cautious side than sorry.

There are two dimensions to optimism:

1. **Permanence** is about time. Optimists believe bad events are temporary. Pessimists believe that bad events will persist into the future. Optimists believe good events will continue. Pessimists believe good events will not last.

2. **Pervasiveness** is about space. Pervasiveness can be specific or universal. Problems can be seen as specific and solvable or universal and unsolvable. Pessimists believe that problems are universal and unsolvable. Optimists believe problems are specific and solvable.

"The best years of your life are the ones in which you decide your problems are your own. You do not blame them on your mother, the ecology or the president. You realise that you control your own destiny."
– Dr. Albert Ellis

OPTIMISTS LIVE LONGER AND ARE HEALTHIER

Optimists are happier, healthier and more successful. People who are optimistic and friendly may have healthier hearts and less chance of heart trouble than the pessimistic and shy. Optimists are healthier because their sense of well-being compels them to engage more actively and persistently with life issues. Research shows that people who express positive emotions come down with fewer colds and flu after being exposed to viruses than those who express negative emotions like, anger, sadness or stress. They tend to be calm, prudent, sensible and resilient. The results of numerous studies of patients with life-threatening diseases, such as AIDS, suggest that those who remain optimistic show symptoms later and survive longer than patients who do not.

Optimists live longer and give better performance at work. In a study of nuns in a USA convent, optimistic nuns were found to live longer. An analysis of autobiographical data showed that those nuns who expressed the most positive emotions in their twenties about their religious vocation were more likely to be alive sixty years later. One study surveyed young people with positive and negative emotions at age 18 and again at 26. Those with positive emotions at 18 were found to be more successful at 26. They were more financially independent, had more career success and had jobs that provided them with greater job satisfaction. Pessimists tended to suffer higher blood pressure, a weakened immune system and slower recovery after major surgery.

"Everybody in the world is seeking happiness – and there is only one sure way to find it. That is by controlling your thoughts. Happiness doesn't depend on outward conditions. It depends on inner conditions." – **Dale Carnegie**

MINDLESS OPTIMISTS

On the other hand, mindless optimism can lead to self-delusion, compulsive gambling and inappropriate decisions. The compulsive gambler is a perpetual optimist who always believes that they will win the next time. It was mindless optimism that induced people to get on the property ladder in 2006 in the belief that property prices only went up and that negative equity was a fable, even though many economists were warning otherwise.

Mindless optimists are less likely to engage in preventative healthcare and to seek medical help when they should. They tend to engage in unsafe sex as they believe that it is only other people who get sexually transmitted diseases. In an organisation, overly optimistic senior managers may ignore economic warning signs and thus fail to take corrective action. The ideal attitude is a judicious mix of optimism with a dash of pessimism so that we do not become too complacent. We should have enough realism to be able to determine between those things we can control from those we cannot.

"Never think that you're not good enough. A man should never think that. People will take you very much at your own reckoning." – **Anthony Trollope**

EMPOWERING BELIEFS

Happiness is a self-fulfilling prophecy. The attitude you have today largely determines how things will turn out tomorrow. Realistic optimists know that things just don't happen fortuitously; you've got to plan ahead and make them happen. They are prepared to move out of their comfort zone to get things done. The more you think failure, the more likely you are to fail. The more you actually fail, the more you expect to fail. You want to fill your mind with empowering beliefs rather than dis-empowering beliefs. The theory of multiple intelligences suggests that we have the basic ability to do almost anything we want, provided we have a good basic intelligence and a self-belief to make it happen.

Empowering beliefs include:

- Everything happens for a purpose. Disappointments are a natural part of life. Try to see the positive aspects of even tragic events in your life.

- We can do anything we want to do, if it interests us enough and we have the determination and persistence to stick to the task until we succeed. If we don't know how to do something we can learn.

- Look at mistakes and failures as stepping stones to success and greater understanding. There is no such thing as failure, only learning. Learn from your mistakes and the feedback you get from them. Adopt the attitude that life is a cycle of continuous improvement.

- Whatever happens, act like an adult and take responsibility for your actions and mistakes. Avoid the blame culture. Nobody expects you to be infallible.

- Family and friends are your greatest resource. Exploit this resource by tapping into the experience and natural creativity and ingenuity of people around you. Don't be afraid to ask questions as questions are our greatest source of learning.

- Realise that you can't change other people or the world, but you can change yourself. As Gandhi said, "become the change you want to see in other people".

- Prosperity is a state of mind and is a relative concept. Some people with very little and a positive attitude to life are more prosperous than others who are very wealthy but disillusioned.

- There is no success without commitment and hard work. Getting ahead in life is not going to be easy. Are you willing to put in the effort and pay the price?

"Life is an endless, truly endless struggle. There's no time when we are going to arrive at a plateau where the whole thing gets sorted. It's a struggle in the way every plant has to find its own way to stand up straight. A lot of the time it's a failure. And yet it's not a failure if some enlightenment comes from it." - Arthur Miller

---

Like success, failure can become a self-fulfilling prophecy. Realistic optimists know that they will sometimes fail but they are not afraid to dust themselves off and start all over again. Optimism is needed when life gets hard and teaches you to become self-sufficient and self-reliant. Optimists are self-empowering, anticipate problems and when unforeseen obstacles arise they are prepared to knuckle down and set in course a plan to overcome them.

"When one door closes another door opens, but we so often look so long and so regretfully upon the closed door, that we do not see the ones which open for us."
– Alexander Graham Bell

COUNTERACTING PESSIMISM

When you think about past experiences you should focus mainly on positive events. There is a natural tendency to dwell on unhappy events in the past. We have been primed by evolution to think negative thoughts and to worry. Examples of negative attitudes include pessimism, worry, envy, apathy, procrastination, and rejection. All of these can undermine a person's confidence and ability to succeed. Experiments show that we remember failures more vividly than successes. When life runs smoothly we're on autopilot. We are only in a state of true consciousness when we notice the stone in our shoe. This tendency to think negatively helped us survive in a dangerous world. Of the six universal emotions, four – anger, fear, disgust and sadness – are negative. The fifth one, joy, is positive. The sixth one, surprise, is neutral. Negative emotions alert us to the fact that something bad has happened and suggests a specific course of action. Anger prompts us to deter aggressors. Fear warns us that danger is near. Disgust urges us to avoid contamination while sadness warns us to be cautious and conserve energy.

People who worry find it difficult to handle uncertainty. The more you are able to tolerate uncertainty the less worried you will be. Thought flooding is a technique recommended by psychologists to neutralise worries. Flooding your mind with thoughts about uncertainty helps you recognise that you can live with ambiguity. Eventually you will realise that continuing to worry is a total waste of time. It's like people who are afraid to go into elevators. If people face up to their fears and do it any-way, eventually the fear will disappear as it has become routine.

> **"A pessimist only sees the dark side of the clouds, and mopes; a philosopher sees both sides and shrugs; an optimist doesn't see the clouds at all – he's walking on them." – Leonard L. Levinson**

Never end with a negative thought. Separate the past from the present and focus more on the present. Mindfulness is all about experiencing and savouring the present moment. Be grateful for the past, hopeful about the future and content with the present. If you spend your time worrying about the past and about the future, then you'll have no time to enjoy the present. Instead of concentrating on the worst possible outcomes, think about the good things that are likely to happen. It's more important to act like an optimist than think like one. The more you act like an optimist the more likely you are to become one.

DISPUTING NEGATIVE THOUGHTS

Simply put, negative thoughts will make you unhappy while positive thoughts will make you happy. You can't always be happy but within reason it does pay to think positively. There is a well-known psychological method of disputing negative thoughts called the ABCDE approach. This is not a new idea but goes back to a Stoic philosopher, Epictetus, who suggested that it is not events, but our beliefs about them, that cause us suffering. You can learn to challenge fearful thoughts and nega-tive assumptions. ABCDE is made up of five stages:

1. **A**dverse event. During the next adverse event in your life, listen to your internal dialogue or self-talk. Is it all gloom and doom? Is this justified?

2. **B**eliefs. Listen carefully and objectively to your beliefs. Are they rational and true? Beliefs have been ingrained from childhood.

3. **C**onsequences. Observe the consequences of your beliefs. Do you feel sad? Do you feel disappointed?

4. **D**ispute. This will interrupt the cycle of pessimism and self-pity. Are your beliefs factual and accurate? What is the evidence for the belief? We are inclined to think the worst. Most of our worries never materialise. Consider alternative explanations for the adverse event. Think of all the ways you can change the situation in the future.

5. **E**nergise. Observe the energy that occurs when you successfully dispute and deal with the negative belief. Viewing situations logically and objectively will help to protect you from undue pessimism.

"A pessimist sees the difficulty in every opportunity; an optimist sees the opportunity in every difficulty." –
Winston Churchill

SELF-ESTEEM

There is a difference between optimism and self-esteem. Optimism is how you perceive situations while self-esteem is how you evaluate yourself, your feelings of self-worth and self-respect. Both make an important contribution to happiness. Self-esteem can be considered to be the ratio of actual successes to aspirations. High self-esteem people have a self-serving bias. This means that they accept responsibility for their successes and blame their failures on external influences. In western cultures self-esteem is highly valued. This is not the case everywhere. In collective cultures like Japan, negative self-appraisals are taken as a path to self-improvement. Similarly, in Chinese society Confucianism teaches the virtues of emotional restraint, respect for others and subtleness to preserve interpersonal harmony rather than assertiveness and ostentation.

People who like and accept themselves feel good about life in general. They are able to take disappointments, failures and frustrations in their stride. They have a realistic assessment of their own self-worth. People with high self-esteem find it easier to cope with the fact that life is difficult and constantly changing and that we do not know what the future holds. Even people with high self-esteem may lose their jobs in times of recession, but high self-esteem people will take it as an opportunity to ask themselves if the job was what they really wanted to do.

> *"To establish true self-esteem we must concentrate on our successes and forget about the failures and the negatives in our lives."* – Denis Waitley

Part of our self-esteem is based on the sense of how likable we are so it's important to surround ourselves with people who respect and admire us. Living up to their high expectations will reinforce our sense of self-worth. However, people with high self-esteem don't rely totally on others' approval, but possess an inherent belief in their own abilities. They don't feel they need everybody to like them. They trust their intuition and are true to themselves, exploit their talents and commit to their own values, ideals and dreams.

Self-Efficacy

Self-efficacy is an important aspect of self-esteem. It is concerned with our confidence or judgement, about our personal capabilities and competencies to successfully execute a specific task within a given context. It is our belief about whether or not we can perform a particular task, bring about a successful outcome or desired results and generally cope with life's challenges. The more we expect to be successful, the more likely we are to take the necessary actions to be successful. Those who feel competent and confident about achieving goals are happier than those who don't. Those with high self-efficacy expect to succeed while those with low self-efficacy expect to fail. In addition, experiencing success raises self-efficacy. However, having low self-efficacy may give you the incentive to research a particular subject and improve your skills.

We develop self-efficacy through self-development, training, continuous learning, observing others and by pursuing challenging goals. In the workplace, relevant training and suitable on-the-job experience together with positive feedback can help people develop a sense of high self-efficacy. Self-efficacy may be confined to a particular skill or area of knowledge. For example, a systems analyst may have a high sense of self-efficacy about solving an information technology problem but have a low sense of self-efficacy about writing a report to the chief executive explaining how the problem was solved. A person with low self-efficacy will see nervousness as proof of their inability to speak in public, whereas a person with high self-efficacy will see feeling nervous as normal and a help to more effective speaking.

"You have to learn the rules of the game. And then you have to play better than anyone else." – **Albert Einstein**

Narcissism

Narcissism is an extreme form of self-esteem and has been defined as a pervasive pattern of grandiosity, need for admiration, and a lack of empathy. Narcissus was a figure in Greek mythology who spent his days admiring his own reflection in a pool, neglecting everybody else in his life. Narcissistic people have a very high opinion of themselves and an excessive need for admiration and attention. They are self-centred with feelings of self-importance, arrogance, grandiosity, egotism and conceit. They feel entitled to special treatment, are easily offended and keep grudges. They don't make good team players.

We all suffer from a mild touch of narcissism. Studies reveal that most ordinary people secretly think they're better than everyone else. We rate ourselves as more dependable, smarter, friendlier, harder-working, less prejudiced, better drivers and even think we display greater sexual prowess in bed than others. It seems that psychologically healthy people need to twist the world to their advantage just a little bit in order to remain sane.

For example, if we do an exam and do well we congratulate ourselves on how clever we are. In contrast, if we do badly, we'll claim that the test was unfair or poorly written and so the result was not our fault. It appears a mild touch of narcissism helps us get through the trials and tribulations of life without losing face in ourselves and faith in our own abilities.

> *"Whoever loves becomes humble. Those who love have, so to speak, pawned a part of their narcissism."*
> **– Sigmund Freud**

There is a clear difference between self-esteem and narcissism. People with high self-esteem are confident and charming, but also caring and considerate. Narcissists have an inflated view of their talents and abilities and only care about themselves. However, unrealistic self-esteem may lead to narcissism, self-delusion and vanity. In addition, according to conventional wisdom it was thought that criminal behaviour was a symptom of low self-esteem and lack of confidence. Now it is known that bullies, criminals, psychopaths and racists often have high self-esteem. The Nazi war criminals tried at Nuremberg after the Second World War had high self-esteem and most insisted that they just followed orders. In fact, their high self-esteem prevented them from understanding the real nature and effects of the evil they had perpetrated.

SUMMARY

Optimism is the tendency to believe, expect or hope that things will turn out well. Optimists feel good about their selves, look at the bright side of life, see the silver lining in every cloud and focus on what is right rather than what is wrong. They are happier, healthier and more successful. Realistic optimists are prepared to move out of their comfort zone to get things done. They don't wait for things to happen, they make things happen.

Optimists view problems as transient, controllable, specific and solvable. They are more resilient and bounce back quicker from setbacks. Optimists use the ABCDE approach to counteract the fallout from adverse events and reframe situations in a more positive light.

Optimism and self-esteem are not the same. Optimism is about how you view situations while self-esteem is about how you view yourself. Both make an important contribution to personal happiness. Narcissism is an unhealthy form of self-esteem. Self-efficacy is our judgement about our capabilities. People with high self-efficacy believe they will succeed within their area of expertise.

Five Activities to Improve Your optimism

1) When you think about bad events in your life view them as temporary, specific and solvable. Think about the lessons you can learn from such experiences and how overcoming them can enrich your life. Then do something positive to move on.

2) Savour and enjoy the present moment. The past has gone and the future is yet to come. All you are guaranteed is the present. Make the most of it.

3) Learn the ABCDE approach to mentally counteract adverse events in your life. This puts you in control of your thoughts rather than be consumed by a sea of negativity.

4) Take life's disappointments, failures and frustrations in your stride. Realise these are part and parcel of living and are a feature of everybody's life. Overcoming them will make you a stronger person. Learn from your mistakes, dust yourself off, and start all over again. Act like an optimist to become an optimist.

5) When you undertake a task, visualise a successful outcome. The anticipation of success will drive you forward to take appropriate actions until the task is completed.

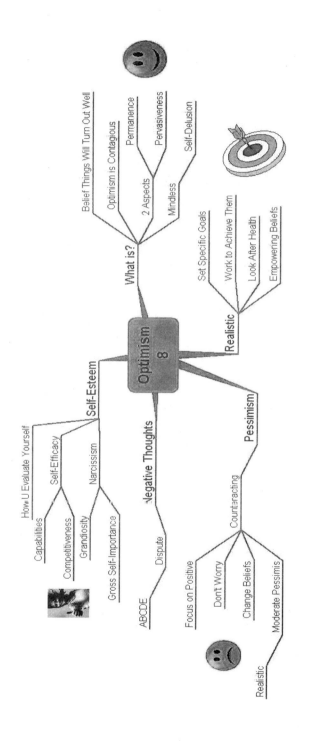

Optimism 8

What is?
- Belief Things Will Turn Out Well
- Optimism is Contagious
- 2 Aspects
  - Permanence
  - Pervasiveness
- Mindless
  - Self-Delusion

Realistic
- Set Specific Goals
- Work to Achieve Them
- Look After Health
- Empowering Beliefs

Self-Esteem
- How U Evaluate Yourself
- Capabilities
- Self-Efficacy
  - Competitiveness
  - Grandiosity
- Narcissism
  - Gross Self-Importance

Negative Thoughts
- ABCDE
- Dispute

Pessimism
- Counteracting
  - Focus on Positive
  - Don't Worry
  - Change Beliefs
- Moderate Pessimis
  - Realistic

9

Smiling and Laughter

- ❖ **What is a duchenne smile?**
- ❖ **What are the benefits of smiling?**
- ❖ **How is laughter good for your health?**
- ❖ **Why is a sense of humour so important?**
- ❖ **Why is humour important in the workplace?**

INTRODUCTION

Starting the day with a smile will help you get into the right mood. Smiling is the basis for friendship, and laughter is a universal language used by all people in every culture. Laughter is contagious and helps people form and maintain friendships. Laughter is good for your health.

One of the most sought after qualities in a partner is a sense of humour. A well-timed joke can defuse a tense situation before it escalates into something nasty. Humour in the workplace helps people to connect, promotes team building and makes people happier. The medieval court jester was used to amuse the king and satirise authority, and political satire is still a feature of modern life. It's well known that men and women have a different sense of humour. Humour is not always positive. Sarcastic and caustic remarks can be hurtful and undermine a relationship.

SMILING

Start your day with a smile and try to maintain a slight smile throughout the day. Consider that the happiest people you know are always smiling or have a pleasant expression on their faces and you will understand the wisdom of this advice. Smiling spreads feelings of goodwill, friendliness, love and care to those you come in contact with. Actions lead to emotions and emotions lead to actions. Smiling can change your attitude and make you feel better. Scientists have found that smiling can activate feelings of happiness. So force a smile the next time you are feeling apprehensive or sad and see the difference it makes.

You can alter your brain chemistry by smiling as smiling sends an endorphin boost to your brain. And remember, it requires 16 muscles to smile but 28 to frown. So use up less energy by smiling! Frowning is more likely to give you wrinkles as smiling tones the muscles in your face which gives you another reason to smile. Women smile more often than men. However, women are more likely to be deceived by a fake smile. Research shows women detect a false smile only 67 per cent of the time while men do so 76 per cent of the time. Babies are born with an innate ability to smile at another human face. A false smile stretches the mouth but never reaches the eyes. You can be trained to give a false smile but a real or genuine smile comes from the heart. A real smile, known in psychology as a duchenne smile, crinkles around the mouth and eyes and is more likely to make people smile in return.

> *"A smile costs nothing, but gives much. Some people are too tired to give you a smile, so give them one of yours. No one needs a smile as much as he who has none to give."* – **Samson Rapheel Hirch**

One of the first steps in making friends is to smile as smiling helps build and support friendships. A smile says I like you and that I'm approachable and friendly. A scowl has the opposite effect. You are more likely to speak to someone who smiles at you as opposed to somebody who has a long sad face. Smiling is contagious and costs nothing. Some people are afraid to smile excessively because they feel they might be seen as a bit silly or mad. Consider that you are lucky to be able to smile. There are people who cannot smile. Such people suffer from a form of facial paralysis – a condition known as moebius syndrome – which is a destructive social handicap.

"Smiling is infectious,
You can catch it like the flu.
Someone smiled at me today,
And I started smiling too." – Author unknown

LAUGHTER

Laughter is a universal language produced and recognised by people of all cultures. It is part of our genetic programming and happens spontaneously. When started it may be difficult to control. Laughter is good for your health. Pain reduction is one of laughter's promising applications. Rosemary Cogan, a professor of psychology at Texas Tech University, found that subjects who laughed at a funny video or underwent a relaxation procedure tolerated discomfort and pain better than other subjects.

Laughter revs up the immune system, lowers blood pressure and enhances the cardiovascular and respiratory systems. It reduces stress by producing the natural pain killers, serotonin and endorphins. In addition, it reduces the stress chemicals, particularly cortisol. Physical benefits include lessening of tissue inflammation, reduction of pain, relaxation of muscles, suppression of the appetite and enhancement of the immune system. Psychological benefits include a sense of euphoria and relaxation that can counter fear, anger, anxiety and depression. With heart attack patients, laughter therapy lowers blood pressure, counteracts stress and reduces the incidence of arrhythmia. Breast-feeding mothers who laugh increase the levels of the relaxing hormone melatonin in breast milk. Infants with atopic eczema who drink the milk reduce their allergic reactions.

Laughter is a form of internal jogging as it gets the lungs moving and the blood circulating. In his 1979 book *Anatomy of an Illness*, Dr Norman Cousins used laughter therapy to relieve symptoms of a painful spinal disease called ankylosing spondylitis by spending ten minutes a day watching comedy films. It seems that laughter truly is the best medicine. A 1998 film called *Patch Adams* starring Robin Williams was based on the true life story of Hunter Adams, a physician who became famous for his unconventional approach to medicine by advocating laughter as a natural way to heal the body. An old Irish proverb says that a good laugh and a long sleep are the best cures in the doctor's book. If you know a good joke, tell it to your family or friends and you will spread a little happiness about.

Like smiling and yawning, laughter is contagious. People bond through laughter and play as it breaks down social barriers. It's impossible to be annoyed or angry at someone who makes you laugh. When people laugh together they feel more positive towards each other. Females laugh naturally and more frequently than males even though men are the main instigators of humour and there are more male comedians than female. Women are attracted to men who make them laugh. Men tend to like women who laugh in their company. A study of children watching cartoons found that girls laughed more often with boys than with other girls. Pre-school children laugh up to 400 times a day, but by the time they reach adulthood, they laugh a mere 15 times per day. What has happened to the other 385 laughs? Canned laughter may sound artificial but it makes television viewers laugh spontaneously as if part of the live theatre audience.

Humour may help to counteract intense pain. James Rotton, of Florida International University, reported that orthopaedic surgery patients who watched comedy videos requested fewer aspirin and tranquilizers than the group that viewed dramas. Humour may also help to reduce tension. In a study by Michelle Newman, an assistant professor of psychology at Penn State University, subjects viewed a film about three gruesome accidents. They then had to narrate it either in a humorous or serious style. Those who used humour had the lowest level of tension. A 2001 letter in the *Journal of the American Medical Association* by Hajime Kimata from Japan reported his findings that allergy patients who watched *Modern Times*, a Charlie Chaplin film, experienced reduced swelling of skin welts.

"Man is the only animal that laughs and weeps; for he is the only animal that is struck with the difference between what things are, and what they ought to be."
– William Hazlitt

Even forced laughter is good for you. Just like smiling the positive effects of laughter are felt whether or not the laughter is real or fake. It increases your endorphin levels and makes you feel relaxed and happy. Laughter clubs founded by Dr. Madan Kataria have sprung up throughout the world. The Indian physician founded the first club in Bombay in 1995. There are now more than 2,500 laughter clubs throughout the world. Members stand in a circle while a certified instructor leads the group in some 20 different laughs. Kataria maintains that to laugh without reason is good for your health. It helps to bond and relax people and relieves tension. Members report that they find it very funny just to watch others laugh. People laugh 30 times more frequently in social than solitary situations. They are more likely to talk to themselves or smile when alone – all the more reason to seek out company and laugh with others. Playfulness, a group setting, and a positive emotional atmosphere mark the social settings of most laughs. Why not try to put more laughter back into your life? Instead of complaining about life's frustrations, why not laugh at the incongruities of life?

HUMOUR AT PLAY

The word "humour" is a Latin derivation originally meaning fluid and flexible. Ancient theories of medicine refer to the four principle humours or fluids in the body. These were called phlegm, blood, black bile and yellow bile. While a balance of these made for good health, an imbalance was seen to create bad health. Too much phlegm made a person cool or apathetic. A large quantity of blood made a person sanguine or cheerful and energetic. An excess of black bile would make a person melancholic or depressive. Finally, too much yellow bile made for an easily angered temperament.

One of the most sought after and desired qualities in a partner is a sense of humour. People with a sense of humour don't take themselves or life too seriously. Humour, however, is very much in the eye of the beholder. It is inherently ambiguous and hence its attraction and danger. A well intended witty remark may be misunderstood in the wrong context. Nevertheless, humour in certain situations allows you to try out ideas and change or withdraw them if they're not well received. It's a way of testing the waters by exploring attitudes to issues.

> *"Humour is the great thing, the saving thing. The minute it crops up, all our irritation and resentments slip away, and a sunny spirit takes their palace."* –
> **Mark Twain**

The medieval court jester was used to amuse the king and satirise authority. Political satire is still a feature of modern life. The expression of political satire is part of the right to freedom of speech and is part of the democratic way of life. Comedians openly joke about the incompetence of government on the television and radio without any dire repercussions. This was not always so. Totalitarian and communist states do not tolerate political satire. When Hitler became chancellor of Germany in 1933 he outlawed anti-Reich jokes as a criminal offence. Satirical books were censored, banned and burnt. Political jokes were considered a direct attack on the state and perpetrators were arrested, imprisoned and in some cases even killed. The controls had the opposite effect with anti-government jokes being expressed in private and in art, poetry and cabaret routines. It seems humans have a tenacious desire for humour.

When you get along with somebody and feel relaxed in their company you are less likely to take offence or get upset at a tease. It's well-known that men and women have a different sense of humour. Men like jokes and slapstick better than women, while women tend to find more humour in collaborative storytelling. Men's humour is also frequently sexual and explicit while women's is less so. Humour can trigger creativity by providing a new perspective on a problem. Humour can help you cope with and survive the worst situations that life can throw at you. It can act as an antidote to stress.

"Good humour is a tonic for mind and body. It is the best antidote for anxiety and depression. It is a business asset. It attracts and keeps friends. It lightens human burdens. It is the direct route to serenity and contentment." **– Grenville Kleiser**

However, humour is not always positive. Sarcastic humour and caustic remarks can be hurtful and undermine a relationship. In years gone by, deformed people were often employed in circuses and fairgrounds for the amusement of the general public. This is no longer acceptable. The film *The Elephant Man* is a good reminder of how people in the past used to pay to go and stare and laugh at people with disfigurements. Jokes about disability, race and other matters can be offensive to the beliefs of others and are not acceptable. On the other hand, self-deprecating humour, since it doesn't hurt anyone else except the deliverer, is funny rather than offensive.

HUMOUR AT WORK

In the workplace humour is now seen as something that helps workers to be happier. Ben and Jerry, the US ice cream company, have established a "joy committee" offering grants to improve workplace happiness. Kodak has created a 1,000 square foot "humour room" for employees to take a "fun break", while at Sun Microsystems, April fool's day pranks are positively encouraged. In the UK, the National Health Service created a "Laughter Clinic" in 1991 and professional comedians now act as jesters to the sick and elderly. The Meadowhall shopping centre in Sheffield employs clowns to entertain shoppers and trains employees to joke with customers. In 1995 British Airways employed an ex-management consultant as a "corporate jester". Some companies celebrate employee milestones such as birthdays and long service awards by making them into social events accompanied by food and beverages. The sense of fun may be enhanced by using funny props to liven up the workplace environment. Typically, these "fun days" are organised to improve productivity when motivation might otherwise be flagging and absenteeism increasing as employees look forward to the weekend.

Southwest Airlines looks for a sense of humour as a quality in job applicants when they are recruiting staff. They look for people with extroverted personalities who will work hard and have fun at the same time. Southwest Airlines knows that if it is to achieve its core principle, "make flying fun", for its customers, it must make its employees' jobs fun first. It is aware that some people have a fear of flying and anything they can do to relax customers is good for business. Walt Disney, who created the benchmark for good customer service, knew the importance of having fun at work as reflected in his saying, "You don't work for a dollar – you work to create and have fun". Disney worked hard to instil this philosophy in his staff as a core value. He wanted to create a work environment that made people smile. A relaxed, playful, pleasant and fun work-place makes people feel happy and this in turn is transmitted to customers.

Humour may backfire, however, and can have disastrous consequences. The classic case of managerial humour backfiring is that of Gerald Rathner. In 1991 he earned £600,000 per annum as the managing director of his family company, which was the largest jewellery chain in the world with 2,500 outlets, a stock market value of £650 million with profits in 1990 of £120 million. In a speech to the Institute of Directors, he joked about the "total crap" of some of the products sold in his stores. Heavily criticised by the tabloid press, Rathner was forced to resign in 1992 and eventually the company had to be sold off. The cost of making inappropriate remarks in the wrong context can be very high.

"Humour is that which most efficiently recognises that we are living in an imperfect world, with imperfect arguments and things that are insane, illogical, and irrational. And the only way we can live with that fact is to laugh." – Anonymous

---

History of Humour

Humour in the workplace was not always seen in a positive light. Managers in the Ford Motor Company in the 1930s and 1940s viewed laughter as a disciplinary offence. They prohibited workers at the River Rouge plant from talking with colleagues, even during work breaks, and treated humming, whistling or even smiling on the job as evidence of soldiering or insubordination. In 1940, John Gallo was sacked because he was caught smiling after committing an earlier breach of laughing with co-workers and slowing down the assembly line by half a minute. This was an extreme example of the scientific management approach in operation.

Attempts to suppress and censor humour and laughter can be traced back much further. Those in charge of the early medieval monasteries, for example, advocated silence. They saw laughter as obscene and sinful and a serious violation of their rules. In ancient Greece a number of social groups like the Pythagoreans, the Spartans and the ascetic Christians were known to oppose laughter. The Greek philosophers Plato and Aristotle argued that amusement caused people to lose control of their reason and thus to act in a less than human way. In his own school, the Academy, Plato prohibited laughter. Aristotle associated excessive laughter with vulgarity, lewdness and the lower classes.

"And we should consider every day lost on which we have not danced at least once. And we should call every truth false which was not accompanied by at least one laugh." – **Friedrich Nietzsche**

SUMMARY

Start your day with a smile and smile frequently during the day. It will put you in a positive mood, help you feel happy and help others smile too. Smiling is infectious and helps build and support friendships. You are more likely to speak to somebody who smiles at you.

Laughter is a universal language used by people of all cultures. Laughter improves our tolerance for pain and is good for our health. Like smiling and yawning laughter is contagious. People bond through laughter and play as it breaks down barriers. It is difficult to be angry at someone who makes you laugh.

One of the most sought after qualities in a partner is a sense of humour. A well-timed joke can defuse an otherwise potentially explosive situation. Humour has been used in the workplace to increase productivity and create a happier workplace.

<u>Five Activities to Improve Your happiness</u>

1) Make it your business to smile frequently throughout the day. It will relax you, make you happy and attract friendships.

2) Take every opportunity to laugh at the incongruities of life.

3) Seek out humorous companions that will encourage you to have a laugh.

4) Learn to tell jokes, have fun and be playful.

5) When brainstorming use humour to generate new perspectives on problems.

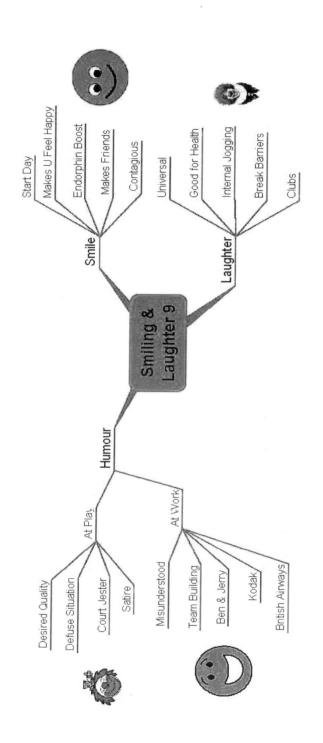

Smiling & Laughter 9

Humour
- At Play
  - Desired Quality
  - Defuse Situation
  - Court Jester
  - Satire
- At Work
  - Misunderstood
  - Team Building
  - Ben & Jerry
  - Kodak
  - British Airways

Smile
- Start Day
- Makes U Feel Happy
- Endorphin Boost
- Makes Friends
- Contagious

Laughter
- Universal
- Good for Health
- Internal Jogging
- Break Barriers
- Clubs

10

LOOKING AFTER YOURSELF

❖ *Why is health so important to happiness?*

❖ *How do you ensure a good nights' sleep?*

❖ *What are the benefits of walking?*

❖ *Why are religious people happier?*

❖ *Why do you need to relax?*

INTRODUCTION

Mental health is more important to your happiness than physical health. Worry and depression are major contributors to unhappiness. A good night's sleep is essential to health and happiness. Sleep deprivation can make you tired and irritable, unable to cope with everyday problems and can impair your physical well-being. Walk your way to health. You are what you eat, so a good diet is essential for health and happiness.

Spirituality is a belief in something greater than us without necessarily adhering to a formal religion. Religion provides social support, a sense of purpose and meaning for our existence and is good for health and happiness. We need recreation as an antidote from the trials and tribulations of everyday life and work. Practising meditation will bring feelings of inner peace, calm and joy.

HEALTH

There is an old saying that your health is your wealth. A wealthy but unhealthy man would spend all his riches to acquire good health. It is impossible to enjoy your wealth if you are very sick. We take our health for granted until we become sick and then we would do anything to have it restored again. Experts maintain that on average smoking one packet of cigarettes a day takes three years off your life. Mental health is more important to your happiness than physical health, although physical health is clearly important too. Depressed people are unable to enjoy life. Most surveys on happiness state that good health is a major contributory factor to happiness. We are lucky to be living at a time when advances in medicine have kept us healthier, prolonged our lives and made us more tolerable. Consider the fate of the first person to be given penicillin. He was an Oxford policeman, named Albert Alexander, who, in 1940, had scratched himself on a rose thorn and developed septicaemia. After he was given the experimental drug, he began to recover, but the supply ran out after five days and he relapsed and died. This was the world before modern medicine.

If you are happy you are less likely to acquire a physical or mental illness than those who are unhappy. Anxiety and depression is a major contributor to unhappiness, especially in the developed world. Many who go for medical help have no physical symptoms but may have mental and psychological problems. Some people are just lonely and want somebody to listen to their concerns. The perception we have of our health is influenced by personality, education, past experience and current emotional state. Our physical health deteriorates with age but the degree and speed of decline varies from person to person. Some people remain healthy into ripe old age.

"He who has health has hope. And he who has hope has everything." – **Arabian proverb**

SLEEP

The average person needs eight hours sleep per day and this is equivalent to spending about a third of our lives asleep. The quality of sleep you have is also important. A restful night's sleep is the ideal. You are exceptional if you can manage with less than eight hours, although Margaret Thatcher, former Prime Minister of England, was reputed to have survived on about four hours per night. Sleep affects our mood and influences our level of happiness. Many people suffer from a sleep deficit, with resulting fatigue, diminished alertness, and gloomy moods. Healthy sleep must contain REM periods – times in which you dream. This is why alcohol-induced sleep is not restful because it interferes with the REM pattern.

One theory maintains that dreams help us rehearse real-life dangerous events so that when we are actually confronted with them we can deal with them more successfully. It's a type of mental rehearsal. Another theory thinks that dreams help us solve problems and come up with creative solutions.

> *"It is a common experience that a problem difficult at night is resolved in the morning after the committee of sleep has worked on it."* – **John Steinbeck**

Many people have been inspired by their dreams. One who did was a German chemist named Friedrich August Kekule. He struggled to find the molecular structure of benzene until he dreamed about a snake devouring its own tail and realised that benzene was a closed circle – a ring. The self-taught Indian mathematician Srinivasa Ramanujan came up with every one of his proofs in dreams. Paul McCartney of the Beatles dreamed the song *Yesterday*, woke up, and wrote it down.

Dreams may help us integrate and consolidate knowledge. During sleep, our brains are making sense of the world, discovering new associations among existing memories, looking for patterns, formulating rules and even solving problems. Our brain creates meaning by putting things together. It helps us make sense of our experiences during our waking hours.

"No day is so bad it can't be fixed with a nap." – Carrie Snow

---

Sleep deprivation can make us tired, irritable and emotionally fragile, unable to cope with everyday problems and to work effectively. People eat more after a few consecutive nights of poor sleep. On top of that, sleep-deprived people exercise less and don't burn off the extra calories. It is not surprising that sleep deprivation is used as a form of torture on political prisoners in some countries and was commonly used to break down captured enemy soldiers during the Second World War. Shift workers whose normal biological circadian rhythms are disrupted because of night work suffer mood swings over the day.

EXERCISE

In the modern developed world most people claim that they have no time to exercise. With so many demands on their time, for many people walking is viewed as a waste of time rather than as a way of keeping fit and healthy. Moderate exercise like walking will add to your lifespan. It provides an opportunity to get extra oxygen into the brain and increases circulation to the heart. It boosts the activity of mood-enhancing neurotransmitters such as dopamine and serotonin and triggers the release of endorphins – morphine-like chemicals that blunt pain and foster relaxation. Studies show that even 10 minutes of vigorous exercise (producing a pulse rate of 100 to 120 beats per minute, depending on your age) can raise endorphin levels for an hour. For those who don't like walking, good alternatives would include dancing, cycling, golfing and swimming. People who start exercise programmes on their own are more likely to give up, compared to those who exercise with one or more partners. When exercise is prolonged and too intense, your immunity system weakens and you are more likely to succumb to illness. For example, marathon runners often get colds and their immune systems may be compromised for weeks or months after a race.

Exercise promotes the growth of brain cells in the hippocampus – the part of the brain associated with memory and learning. Walking thus improves our capacity to memorise, learn, concentrate and do abstract reasoning. Walk your way to health. Invest in a pedometer which measures the number of steps you take. Take about 10,000 steps each day or about five miles at a moderately vigorous pace to keep reasonably fit.

"Those who think they have no time for bodily exercise will sooner or later have to find time for illness."
– Edward Stanley

Those who are reluctant to take up walking should get themselves a dog. After all, a dog is a man's best friend and a great source of joy and happiness for some! Dogs need exercise and will encourage you to do likewise. You now have an excuse for going for a walk. You will also get an opportunity to meet others out walking their dogs that will be only too willing to exchange information about their pets. Research suggests that pet owners live longer and tend to be more optimistic and suffer from less stress. Owning a dog will also reduce loneliness and depression, and will lower your blood pressure and cholesterol.

Benefits of Walking

There are many benefits of walking. It costs nothing, unlike going to a gym, and can be done every day weather permitting. Develop the daily routine of walking so that if you don't walk you miss it. If you walk 15 minutes it uses up the same number of calories as running the same distance in 8.3 minutes. If you walk two miles a day three days a week you can reduce your weight by one pound every three weeks. Every minute you walk may add up to two minutes to your life.

Walking is particularly good for people suffering from depression, anxiety or stress. It is an antidote to sadness because it promotes vitality and a positive mood and may act as a diversion from negative thoughts. It helps people get a restful night's sleep and blocks pain. It is a good insurance against premature ageing. Active older people suffer less cognitive decline than sedentary ones, and aerobic exercise such as walking will keep you sharper at any age. Swimming is not as accessible as walking but for those near the sea or indoor swimming facilities it is an excellent alternative. Swimming is a great way of keeping in shape as it tones the muscles.

"The only exercise some people get is jumping to conclusions, running down their friends, side-stepping responsibility, and pushing their luck!" – Author unknown

---

For the more active, sport offers many opportunities for enjoyment, exercise and making friends. Even indoor sports such as table tennis or badminton can keep you active during those dark winter nights. Golfing has a social dimension and can be enjoyed at any age and will keep you reasonably fit. Sport provides occasions for social contact and family outings. It improves skills by improving coordination and increases self-esteem.

DIET

You are what you eat. Even our moods are linked to what we eat. As well as being a source of nutrients, food is a basic pleasure and a source of happiness. It is also an excuse for getting together socially with family and friends. An adequate diet is very important to your health. For best results, keep to regular mealtimes. Don't skip your breakfast as it is the most important meal of the day. People who skip breakfast may overeat at lunch. Snacking and eating in between meals is a contributory factor to obesity.

Fish is the best brain food available so you should eat fish a few times a week. Omega-3 polyunsaturated fatty acids found in fish are essential for keeping your brain in tip-top shape. A 2006 study by researchers at the University of Pittsburgh School of Medicine found that people who eat fish are not only happier, but tend to have more pleasant personalities than people who don't eat fish. People who don't eat fish are more likely to report mild symptoms of depression, feelings of impulsivity and a negative outlook on life. Eat sufficient protein and five portions of vegetables/fruit daily. Don't gulp down food but instead savour the taste to enjoy the process of eating and help digestion. Avoid junk food such as cakes, soft drinks, sweets, crisps and biscuits as they pile on the calories.

> *"Don't dig your grave with your own knife and fork."*
> **– English proverb**

Obesity is one of the main killers in the developed world and is now even affecting children. There is an abundance of food available and people eat too much. We are constantly bombarded by advertisements to eat this or that product. Obesity is a major cause of diabetes even in very young people. In older people obesity can cause cancer and heart disease. Many people are in a state of denial regarding obesity. The Nutrition and Health Foundation research in 2007 found a large degree of complacency with some 16 per cent of the group surveyed classified as obese, yet only 9 per cent admitted to being significantly overweight. Men were less likely than women to try any kind of diet or exercise change. Support of family and friends is essential to the success of any diet or exercise programme undertaken. In addition to overeating, lack of exercise, often due to too much television viewing, is a major contributory cause for obesity.

SPIRITUALITY

The word spirituality comes from the Latin root *spiritus*, or breath – referring to the breath of life. It involves opening your heart to feelings of wonder, reverence and gratitude. You can be spiritual without being religious. You may believe in something greater than yourself without adhering to a formal religion. Most of us like to know how our life fits into the greater scheme of things. We are being spiritual when we wonder where the world came from, why we are here and where we go when we die. The human need for things spiritual is amply evidenced by the number of books on spirituality in the bookshops, some of which have become best sellers. In addition, CDs of Gregorian chants by monks top the charts from time to time. In times of recession people tend to turn to God and spirituality.

Religions in their different ways answer these questions. All the major religions preach positive ideas like acting ethically and morally, being truthful and honest, treating people equally, with respect and kindness, and practising charity and avoiding self-ishness. These are all precepts for good living and if people practised them there would be very little trouble in the world. Obviously, though, you don't have to be religious to practise good principles of living.

In the workplace, spiritual managers are more likely to be concerned about the human health and well-being of their employees and thus create more humane and socially responsible organisations. They are more likely to adopt moral philosophies that emphasise the virtues of truth, honesty, authenticity, humility, respect and service to others. They are more likely to walk the talk and act as role models for the ethical values, attitudes and behaviour necessary for a successful organisation.

"The possession of knowledge does not kill the sense of wonder and mystery. There is always more mystery." – **Anais Nin**

Religion is Good for Your Health

Research over many years has shown that religion is good for your health. Religion gives people a reason to focus beyond the self, and a timeless perspective on the trials and tribulations of life. Religions teach people to avoid risky behaviours like excessive drinking and eating, drug abuse, gambling and illicit sex. Religion provides people with an opportunity to practise short meditative acts. Meditation has been shown to have a strong link with well-being because it calms the mind, provides a diversion away from problems, reduces stress and anxiety, and supports positive thinking. Those who take part in church ceremonies are less stressed over finance, health and other daily concerns than nonspiritual people. Those who pray or read the Bible regularly experience lower blood pressure than non-practising peers.

The children of religious families feel more secure because they tend to have more stable relationships within and outside the family. An extensive survey in 2008 in the USA by the Associated Press and MTV found that people aged 13 to 24 who describe themselves as very spiritual or religious tend to be happier than those who don't. Sociologists have long drawn a connection between happiness and the sense of community and support inherent to most religious practice. They are also remarkably tolerant about other religious or spiritual beliefs. People who believe in God and in an afterlife have a lower fear and anxiety about death. Christians believe that true happiness is not experienced in this world but rather in the hereafter when we are reunited with God.

"The most beautiful thing we can experience is the mysterious. It is the source of all true art and all science. He to whom this emotion is a stranger, who can no longer pause to wonder and stand rapt in awe, is as good as dead: his eyes are closed." **– Albert Einstein**

Most religions believe in a life after death. Even the ancient Egyptians had a strong belief in the afterlife and went to considerable trouble to prepare their tombs for their death. The Pharaohs built pyramids as a passage to the next world and to ensure their immortality. Their bodies were preserved and they were buried surrounded by their worldly riches.

The downside of religion is the misguided feeling of some adherents that their brand of religion is superior to others and is the one true faith. This can lead to intolerance and hatred and, in the case of some fundamentalists, misguided terrorism in the form of suicide bombers. They are indoctrinated to see their acts as noble, morally justified and acts of supreme self-sacrifice.

The Seven Deadly Sins

The Christian religions teach their followers to avoid the seven deadly sins of lust, gluttony, greed, sloth, wrath, envy and pride. The opposite of the seven deadly sins are the virtues of chastity, temperance, charity, diligence, patience, kindness and humility. Studies suggest that religious people live longer and are happier. This is not surprising as they are taught to cultivate the virtues of love, tolerance, compassion, gratitude, kindness and caring for others. Religion gives them a sense of identity and support in troublesome times like bereavement.

RECREATION

We need recreation to distract us from our everyday routine of domesticity and work. Recreation and leisure can be a source of happiness. Start a hobby like stamp or coin collecting. Read widely about your interest and become an expert in the field. Being busy at a hobby is preferable to being bored and will keep your mind occupied and challenged. With a hobby you will always have something to do in your spare time. Some people have even turned their hobbies into profitable pursuits and even full-time jobs.

"Life is best enjoyed when time periods are evenly divided between labour, sleep and recreation. All people should spend one-third of their time in recreation which is rebuilding, voluntary activity, never idleness." **– Brigham Young**

Travelling to foreign countries is a great source of enjoyment while enriching you at the same time. Holidays are also good for your health. Research done at the State University of New York and the University of Pittsburgh show that those who take annual vacations are 20 per cent less likely to die in the next nine years. It is well known that holidays are a remedy for stress, as escaping from a familiar environment and being challenged by a new country with its own landscape, language, art, architecture, history and culture will distract you from everyday worries and stimulate your brain cells. Going on holidays with your friends or family will also help to cement relationships.

Get more enjoyment from music. Notice the way it can create sadness at a funeral or feelings of joy at a wedding. It can create moods of solemnity at a church service or excitement at a military parade. Music can be used as a way to relax and create feelings of great joy and happiness. For example, a fast tempo creates feelings of happiness or energy. A slower tempo may create tranquil and sentimental feelings. Consonant harmonies are playful and happy while dissonant harmonies seem more ominous and sad. When you are feeling down, use the appropriate music to lift your spirits and give you a renewed zest for life.

"It's just such a freeing thing to set these great challenges for yourself, to travel, to learn more about the world, to just go out there and get crazy and get free and get strong." – **Angelina Jolie**

MEDITATION

Meditation has now become popularised in Western culture. However, meditation is not a new technique for achieving peace and tranquillity. Buddhists have practised meditation for centuries while monks and nuns in Christian monasteries have tried to achieve happiness by meditation, contemplation and prayer and by withdrawal from the world. Tai Chi is a type of meditation developed by Taoist monks to promote healing. Combining movement, meditation and special breathing, the practice has been linked to a lower risk of heart disease, fewer falls in the elderly and enhanced mood. Meditation is about emptying your brain of everyday mental clutter and distractions by concentrating on one thought. It's about learning to quiet the mind. Slow down and allow yourself time to be silent and calm. Meditation gives you an opportunity to be alone. From time to time everybody needs to be alone for reflection and quietness. A simple way to meditate is to concentrate on your breathing for about 20 minutes daily. Sit in a comfortable chair with your back straight. Stop all thoughts and forget about your problems. Relax your muscles. Breathe in and out through your nostrils to the count of four. Concentrate totally on each in and out breath. Meditation is about giving attention to one thing at a time. It is impossible to think of two things at the same time. We are thus able to focus attention on what we choose.

Experiments with people who practise meditation like monks show that they generate more left hand activity in the brain and have more control over their emotions. They are in control of their thoughts rather than their thoughts being in control of them. They focus attention longer and show more compassion and empathy than people who don't practise meditation. People who practise meditation have more gamma waves in their brain than novices. This suggests that the brain can be trained to be happier.

"Prayer is when you talk to God: meditation is when you listen to God." – **Diana Robinson**

SUMMARY

Your health is your wealth. Sick people would spend all the money and time they have to be healthy again. Sleep affects our mood and influences our level of happiness. A good night's sleep is important for your health and sense of well-being. The brain needs oxygen to survive. Walking provides extra oxygen to the brain and keeps the circulation system healthy. Walking clears the mind and improves our capacity to learn. It keeps us fit, prevents us from becoming obese and gives us a sense of exhilaration and joy.

You are what you eat. Even our moods are linked to what we eat. As well as being a source of nutrients, food is a source of pleasure. Keeping to the teachings of your religion will keep you healthy and happy. All the major religions preach positive ideas like acting ethically and morally, treating people equally and with respect, practising charity and avoiding selfishness. These are all precepts for good living and a happy life. Recreation and leisure acts as an antidote to work. Leisure pursuits can be a source of joy and happiness. We need to meditate to clear our minds of mental clutter, discover ourselves and experience feelings of solitude and inner calm.

Five Activities to Improve Your happiness

1) Go to sleep at a regular time each night. For a good night's sleep, before going to bed you should drink hot milk and avoid alcohol and caffeine.

2) Take about 10,000 steps daily or about five miles to keep you healthy and fit. Develop this into a daily routine. Invest in a pedometer to measure the number of steps that you need to reach your quota.

3) Eat a healthy breakfast. Eat sufficient protein and five portions of vegetables/fruit each day, and avoid junk food such as cakes, sweets, soft drinks, crisps and biscuits.

4) Even if you aren't religious adopt the precepts of religion such as acting morally and ethically, treating people equally and with respect, practising charity and avoiding selfishness. These are the foundations for a happy life.

5) Take about 10 minutes to meditate each day. Empty your mind by concentrating on your breathing.

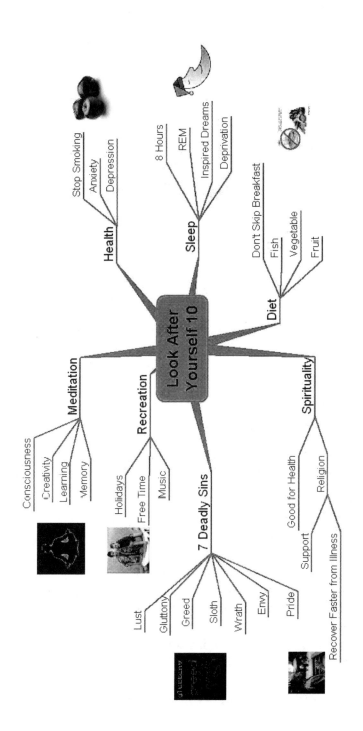

Look After Yourself 10

Health
- Stop Smoking
- Anxiety
- Depression

Sleep
- 8 Hours
- REM
- Inspired Dreams
- Deprivation

Diet
- Don't Skip Breakfast
- Fish
- Vegetable
- Fruit

Meditation
- Consciousness
- Creativity
- Learning
- Memory

Recreation
- Holidays
- Free Time
- Music

7 Deadly Sins
- Lust
- Gluttony
- Greed
- Sloth
- Wrath
- Envy
- Pride

Spirituality
- Good for Health
- Religion
- Support
- Recover Faster from Illness

11

LIFELONG LEARNING

- ❖ Why are lifelong learners happier and more successful in life?
- ❖ Why do novices sometimes make significant discoveries?
- ❖ What are the benefits of education?
- ❖ What is accelerated learning?
- ❖ What is hothousing?

INTRODUCTION

Lifelong learners are happier and more successful in life. They are more likely to make sensible decisions and marry a suitable partner. Novices can often make significant discoveries. They may have a unique perspective and solve problems or do things in a new way that nobody has done before. Education raises levels of happiness by increasing opportunities and income and providing more interesting work.

Modern education is obsessed with measurement. People who fail formal school examinations often develop feelings of inadequacy. A good education provides self-confidence and a sense of control. It broadens the mind and makes you less susceptible to irrational fears and superstitions. Play promotes the development of social and emotional skills including teamwork. Accelerated learning is suitable for adults but a variation called hothousing poses many problems for children.

CHALLENGE OF LIFELONG LEARNING

The love of learning will provide you with a feeling of intrinsic motivation. Lifelong learners are happier and more successful in life. They are naturally curious and want to know how things work. They have better paid jobs and thus enjoy a higher standard of living. They develop their minds by using logic, creativity, problem solving skills and language effectively.

> *"One of the things that may get in the way of people being lifelong learners is that they're not in touch with their passion. If you're passionate about what it is you do, then you're going to be looking for everything you can to get better at it."* – Jack Canfield

Some people give up learning after their formal education and undertake no further formal studies during their lives. The memories of school learning are often of an unpleasant nature and thus something to forget about. Most of our formal education focused on rote learning – hardly a challenge to an inquisitive and creative mind! Rote learning does not tap into a person's interest or satisfy a person's curiosity and therefore is unlikely to engender a passion for learning. The goal of learning should be to understand what is happening around you and to make sense of your experience and of the world. Learning should not be seen as a chore but as challenging, effortless and enjoyable.

DELIGHTS OF DISCOVERY

You don't have to be a professional scientist to make discoveries. Even dedicated amateurs can do so. The challenge to solve a particular problem will drive you on. Novices may have a unique perspective and may solve problems or do things in a way that nobody has done before. People dedicated to playing with ideas over many years often make significant breakthroughs. Many famous scientists were amateurs or made discoveries outside their area of qualification. It was just a passionate interest and innate curiosity that drove them on.

"I have learned the novice can often see things that the expert overlooks. All that is necessary is not to be afraid of making mistakes, or of appearing naïve." – Abraham Maslow

---

Gregor Mendel, an Augustinian priest and the father of modern genetics, published his findings in 1866 but they were not widely accepted until after his death. Luigi Galvani, a physician, discovered some of the laws of electricity in 1791. The galvanometer is named after him. Galileo was a medical doctor and published his findings in 1632 that the sun, not the earth, was the centre of the universe and that the earth moved around the sun and not vice versa.

EDUCATION

Education has an indirect affect on levels of happiness. At any particular age, those with more education are happier than those with less. Happiness is not an explicit aim of education but it is a by-product. It raises levels of happiness by increasing opportunities for more income and for more interesting work. More income provides a better standard of living. Better educated people live longer, probably because they make more informed decisions about their careers, health and lifestyle. Education also opens the mind to possibilities of further education.

Having a high intelligence quotient (IQ) makes little difference to happiness, however having a high emotional quotient (EQ) does. Happiness and EQ are not subjects on the curriculum although many academics think they should be. People can be taught how to improve their EQ. There is some evidence that a good EQ is a predictor of success in life in such areas as satisfaction with life, friendships, family life and occupational success. The Centre for Creative Leadership found that senior executives who were sacked failed because they had EQ deficiencies rather than a lack of technical ability. These included having poor inter-personal relationship skills, being too authoritarian or too ambitious, and creating conflict with upper management.

Similarly, some academics think that children should be taught how to be happy. They claim that teaching children to live happy and independent lives increases the chances of them avoiding depression, mental illness and dependency on others when they become adults. Positive psychologists claim there is increasing evidence of the effectiveness of well-being programmes.

> *"I believe through learning and application of what you learn, you can solve any problem, overcome any obstacle and achieve any goal that you can set for yourself."* – **Brian Tracey**

Modern education is obsessed with measurement in the form of final examinations. People who don't "measure up" often develop feelings of inadequacy and lack of confidence. These feelings are reinforced when comparisons are made with successful students. Education should be more about developing the broader skills such as problem solving, creativity, happiness and emotional intelligence. It should be more about equipping you with learning to learn skills so that you can go on learning for the rest of your life. It should teach you how to be curious, to ask questions and not to accept things at face value.

Benefits of Education

The benefits of a good education include:

- *Social and emotional competence.* On average, girls are more emotionally literate than boys. One expects educated people to be more emotionally aware than uneducated people but there are always exceptions to the rule. Emotional competence is very important for managers who need to be able to control their anger and stress when dealing with difficult employees.

- *Sense of control.* Because educated people are better informed they are more aware of what's going on in the world and therefore more in control of their lives. Even when they don't know something they are in a better position to find out.

- *Resilience.* Educated people have more resources to bounce back after suffering setbacks. They know the systematic approach to solving problems and realise that there are alternative approaches to the solution of every issue.

- *Self-esteem.* Being educated gives a person a sense of self-worth and self-esteem. A person may lose their wealth but cannot lose their education. Once acquired it cannot be lost or taken away from you. Knowledge is always a resource you can fall back on and exploit to your advantage.

- *Education broadens the mind and gives a person an outward focus.* Educated people realise that what they know is only the tiniest fraction of the knowledge available in the world. Will Durant, a US author and historian, said that education was a progressive discovery of our ignorance. Educated people are not afraid to admit what they don't know, to question things and to seek out the relevant source of information.

"The principal goal of education is to create men who are capable of doing new things, not simply of repeating what other generations have done." – Jean Piaget

---

- *Educated people are aware of their personal strengths and weaknesses.* They will exploit their strengths and do everything possible to minimise their weaknesses. They are likely to be lifelong learners.

- *Educated people are less vulnerable to irrational fears and superstitions.* They like to base their decisions on facts rather than hearsay. They are more likely to take a rational view of situations they confront.

- *Educated people tend to engage in purposeful and meaningful activities related to their goals in life.* They prioritise their time rather than waste it. They realise that time is the most precious resource they have. Formal study has taught them how to concentrate and organise their time effectively.

"Wisdom doesn't come with old age. Nothing does – except wrinkles. It's true, some wines improve with age. But only if the grapes were good in the first place." – Abigail Van Buren

---

THE ROLE OF PLAY

The role of play in the development of people should be appreciated. We should concentrate on process, discovery and learning rather than perfection in our every day lives and at work. Civilisation's greatest geniuses, from Leonardo to Einstein, have all understood the value of play and enthusiasm. The Protestant work ethic discourages play and sees work as a serious and necessary chore rather than a source of happiness. People thus look to leisure as a way of compensating for the drudgery of work. The solution is to encourage playfulness in our everyday lives. Enthusiasm is a more powerful motivator than necessity.

Play promotes the development of social and emotional skills including teamwork. Play fosters independent thinking, creativity and communication skills. Play is just as important for adults as it is for children. Play compared to work is intrinsically motivational. The more work becomes like play the more motivational it becomes. Information technology and mobile phones have increased the opportunities for play. Some companies are trying to introduce flexibility and fun into the workplace to make it more enjoyable and less formal.

"The opposite of play isn't work. It's depression. To play it to act out and be wilful, exultant and committed, as if one is assured of one's prospects." – **Brian Sutton-Smith**

ACCELERATED LEARNING

The term accelerated learning was coined by the followers of Dr. Georgi Lozanov, a Bulgarian educator who developed a teaching method known as "suggestology". Children are accelerated learners naturally – they are not experts, but they are expert learners, naturally attentive and inquisitive, and if properly nurtured may continue to learn everything at an accelerated rate. It is well known that very young children find it no problem to learn languages (in the right environment) whereas adults may do so only with difficulty. However, when adults really want to learn something they often experience feelings of childlike wonder and enthusiasm which accelerate their learning. Accelerated learning techniques have been applied successfully to the teaching and learning of foreign languages.

Accelerated learning is about acquiring, understanding, and retaining information quickly, as if returning to that childlike state. It is based on the premise that words when combined with music (especially baroque music) and delivered with emotion are easier to learn. The method involves techniques to relax learners and create a stress-free environment. The method has been used successfully in many areas of training and learning including language and memory training. Accelerated learning has been broadened to include developments in techniques of learning, learning styles, multiple intelligence, study skills, teaching, memorisation, visualisation, speed-reading, chunking, objective setting, Neuro-linguistic programming (NLP) and the use of mind maps.

Hothousing

Accelerated learning is okay for adults but certain forms may not be suitable for some young children. An aggressive variation of the concept, called hothousing, has been advocated to accelerate the educational development of very bright or gifted children. It may, however, stunt their social and emotional development. The results have been mixed. Advocates of the practice claim that it is essential if you want the brightest to develop to their potential. Some universities support talented children in special schools among their peers until they are old enough for university. The National Association for Gifted Children (NAGC) in the UK and Mensa advocate summer schools and clubs to keep prodigies intellectually stimulated.

> *"You need to have a passionate interest in why things are happening. The cast of mind, kept over long periods, gradually improves your ability to focus on reality. If you don't have the cast of mind, you're destined for failure even if you have a high IQ."* – Charlie Munger

Critics maintain that hothousing has a long-term cost. Some child prodigies end up as unhappy and unsuccessful adults. Some are educated by their parents at home and miss out on the social and emotional development which is part and parcel of attending a normal school. Hothousing, if aggressively pursued, may discourage a lifelong love of learning and produce very unhappy and frustrated children. Children learn most when they are enjoying themselves and they need to develop the confidence, self-esteem and self-worth that come from interacting and playing with children of their own age. A child must be sufficiently developed and motivated to learn. Force-feeding education is counterproductive if the child lacks inherent interest. Although these children may be very bright they often lack the maturity which only comes with age and experience.

Gordon Brown, the Prime Minister of England, was chosen for a hothouse education programme but said at 16 that he hated the experiment. However, he was accepted by the University of Edinburgh to study history at the early age of 16 and went on to take on leadership roles in student politics. He is obviously one of the success stories.

Research findings in 2006 by Joseph Mahoney, an associate professor in the psychology department of Yale University in the USA, suggest that children who take part in after-school activities such as drama and football get better exam results. They have a stronger relationship with their parents and are less likely to smoke or drink. They are more competent, better adjusted and less prone to anti-social behaviour such as dropping out of school. It seems to be all a question of balance and common sense. Overburdening children with too many extra curricular activities may only creates anxiety, stress and even burnout. Children need a normal childhood in order to grow up to become well-adjusted adults.

"The illiterate of the 21st century will not be those who cannot read and write, but those who cannot learn, unlearn, and relearn." – **Alvin Toffler**

SUMMARY

The love of learning will help you be happier and more successful in life. Lifelong learners are naturally curious and want to know how things work. They have better paid jobs and enjoy a good standard of living. They are more likely to make sensible decisions in life and marry a suitable partner.

Education raises the level of happiness by increasing opportunities for lucrative employment and for more interesting work. Better educated people live longer because they make more informed decisions about their health and lifestyles. The benefits of education include social and emotional competence and a sense of control. Educated people have more resources to bounce back after suffering setbacks. Education increases self-esteem. The benefits of play include social development and developing the skills of teamwork.

Accelerated learning is fine for adults but may not be suitable for all young children. A variation of accelerated learning called hothousing has been used to accelerate the education of very bright children with mixed results. It seems to be a question of balance. Too many extra curricular activities may only create anxiety, stress and even burnout.

Five Activities to Improve Your happiness

1) Become a lifelong learner. Undertake a programme of reading. Read at least one book a month in your speciality.

2) Become a dedicated amateur in a subject that interests you. It will take about 10 years to become an expert in your chosen subject.

3) Undertake a formal educational programme that will help you progress in your career. There are many part-time educational opportunities available. Distance learning programmes may suit the lifestyle of people who work.

4) Take a course on learning to learn skills so that you can equip yourself to go on learning throughout your life.

5) Do research on accelerated learning and apply the findings to your own learning.

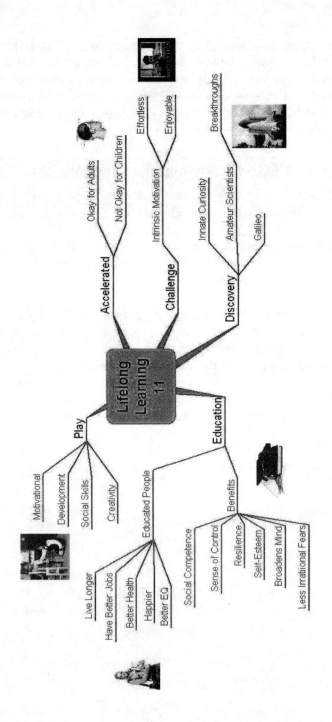

Lifelong Learning 11

Play
- Motivational
- Development
- Social Skills
- Creativity

Accelerated
- Okay for Adults
- Not Okay for Children

Challenge
- Intrinsic Motivation
  - Effortless
  - Enjoyable

Discovery
- Innate Curiosity
- Amateur Scientists
  - Galileo
- Breakthroughs

Education
- Educated People
  - Live Longer
  - Have Better Jobs
  - Better Health
  - Happier
  - Better EQ
- Benefits
  - Social Competence
  - Sense of Control
  - Resilience
  - Self-Esteem
  - Broadens Mind
  - Less Irrational Fears

12

LIVING WITH INTEGRITY

❖ *Why is ethics important to happiness?*

❖ *Why are lying and cheating endemic in society?*

❖ *What is the impact of hypocrisy?*

❖ *Why is individualism bad for society?*

❖ *What is the principle of impartiality?*

INTRODUCTION

An ethical life is a happy life. Ethics is about performing wholesome actions and avoiding unwholesome actions. Trust is the oil that keeps lives in harmony and business functioning smoothly and successfully. When people lie and cheat trust disappears. Malicious gossip is dangerous and can ruin reputations, poison relationships and derail careers as well as causing great personal unhappiness. Hypocrisy is advocating one thing and doing another. To be happy we need to be congruent and adhere to our principles, values and beliefs.

Fraud, greed and corruption have thrived in the banking and corporate sectors because of the loose official scrutiny and regulation of business practices. The rise of individualism and selfishness has been accompanied by the decline in moral, community and religious values. This has created a moral vacuum and a dearth of deference to figures of authority in the West. The opposite of individualism is mutuality of interests and a sense of fairness. People are happiest when they are contributing towards the welfare of others.

ETHICS

An ethical life is a happy life. Ethics is about doing the things you should do to live an honest, happy and successful life. Surveys show that the key ingredients people like in their leaders and their friends are truth, integrity, humanity, honesty and humility.

"Rules cannot take the place of character." – **Alan Greenspan**

Unethical people are frowned on and often shunned by society, especially when they are found out. Some acts are illegal as well as being unethical while some acts are legal but unethical. In such cases the courts will enforce legal contracts and punish crime. In extreme cases people may find themselves in jail for unethical and illegal acts. Sometimes the law and ethics are out of step but eventually the law will catch up and make the unethical acts illegal. Many companies have collapsed because although they were acting within the law they were acting unethically.

Ethics is about performing good actions and avoiding bad ones. It is about performing to the expectations and living up to the accepted principles of a decent society. An ethical society is a happy society. Ethical people act for the benefit of others rather than for their own selfish interests. People of character act with integrity, tell the truth, keep their promises and always do the right thing. My word is my bond is the foundation for good business and good personal relationships. The opposite of integrity is deceitfulness and insincerity. People now realise that statistics and "facts" can be manufactured, manipulated and cherry-picked to suit the presenter. Hence the saying: "lies, damn lies and statistics". Truthfulness, transparency and moral behaviour create respect, trust and attract friendship and goodwill which are important ingredients for a happy life.

> *"Do all the good you can, by all the means you can, in all the ways you can, in all the places you can, at all the times you can, to all the people you can, as long as ever you can."* – John Wesley

People should seek to be fair rather than right. Sometimes a strict interpretation of law may cause too much hardship in certain circumstances. For example, a company in liquidation may walk away from its obligations to creditors. This is legally right but morally wrong. In justice a creditor is still entitled for payment for goods and services supplied. This is where a sense of ethics and fair play comes in. Laws only represent the accumulated wisdom of the past. Additional wisdom may be needed to identify exceptions. People deserve to be paid for out of pocket costs irrespective of the legal situation.

TRUST

Business is run on the basis of trust. People are expected to deal with each other in an honest, respectful, straightforward and cooperative manner. Business would grind to a halt if everything had to be put down in writing. Verbal agreements are the basis of fast, efficient and good business. Ethical people are decent and consistent and so their words should match their actions. There are no hidden agendas. People should put themselves in the other person's shoes. We should have empathy for the other person's needs, problems and suffering.

Trust takes a long time to build up but can be destroyed in an instant. In his 1986 book, *Innovation and Entrepreneurship*, Peter Drucker, the management guru, estimated that building up trust in business takes a minimum of three years. In personal relationships infidelity in marriage breaks the bond of trust and is likely to end the marriage. To safeguard against infidelity and other possibilities some couples draw up a prenuptial agreement – hardly the basis for trust in a marriage as it indicates a lack of trust from the start of the relationship.

The respect and trust in banks has been destroyed by the financial scandals that came to light in 2008 and will be extremely difficult to restore. Banks are hated because nobody trusts them anymore and most have suffered because of their reckless lending. In 2008 we had bankers awarding themselves huge salary increases and bonuses while the banking system was collapsing around their ears. They were rewarding themselves for failure. People facing redundancy, the unemployed and those who saw a devaluation of their pensions resent this selfish and greedy behaviour. Shareholders have seen their shares diminish in value to a tiny fraction of what they were before the crises began while at the same time senior bankers enrich themselves.

"Do not trust all men, but trust men of worth; the former course is silly, the latter a mark of prudence." – **Democritus**

Employees like to work for employers they feel care for them and whom they can trust. Employees will not trust colleagues who bad mouth them and put them down behind their backs. Breaking commitments and not keeping promises is the quickest way to undermine trust. We trust people we can confide in with the assurance that they will not break our confidences. We trust people whom we know will come to our assistance in times of trouble.

A 2005 survey for the World Economic Forum found worldwide declines in trust in the UN, in national governments, non-governmental organisations, multinational corporations and large local companies. In the cases of national governments, the UN and multinational corporations, these trust levels have never been lower. Most of us trust some people more than others. As you can imagine, trust in bankers, lawyers, accountants and estate agents are at an all time low. Trust in doctors, teachers and judges remains relatively high.

> **"Whoever is careless with the truth in small matters cannot be trusted with important matters." – Albert Einstein**

LYING AND CHEATING

People who lie and betray are unlikely to be trusted again. Lies are not acceptable but in certain circumstances white lies may be the better option than the whole truth. In everyday life sometimes white lies are justified when told to avoid hurting people, maintain positive relationships and bring a little joy and happiness into people's lives. Thus it is better, more diplomatic and more sensitive to tell your spouse that you love her new hairstyle or outfit rather than reveal your real opinion and hurt her feelings. It can be acceptable to lie to protect the lives of others. The classic example is the concealment by the family and friends of Anne Franks to protect her from the Nazi concentration camps.

Psychologists claim that people are more likely to tell lies over the telephone than in face to face encounters because it is easier to do so due to lack of body language feedback. Extroverts tend to lie more than introverts because they are eager to please others and win approval.

In general, we are not surprised when members of certain professions tell lies such as politicians, estate agents, marketing people and public relations consultants. False advertising, misleading information and mislabelling are common practices in marketing. PR consultants are hired by politicians to create spin and confusion. We feel especially aggrieved when members of the police, the medical profession or clergy have been found to be telling lies on the basis if we can't trust the police, doctors and clergy who can we trust?

> **"I'm not upset that you lied to me, I'm upset that from now on I can't believe you." – Friedrich Nietzsche**

It seems that politicians find it very difficult to tell the truth, the whole truth and nothing but the truth despite the fact that those who lie often pay a substantial price in terms of their personal reputations, happiness and career. Some politicians are forced to resign when their lies become public knowledge. Straight talking, truthfulness and transparency are not the hallmarks of modern politicians.

Charles Haughey, the Prime Minister of Ireland, continuously lied about the source of his great wealth but was eventually forced to resign in 1992 because of rumours of bribery and corruption which subsequently proved to be true. He was in power when there was widespread corruption, bribery and tax evasion. Banks routinely advised their customers to avoid deposit interest retention tax (DIRT) contrary to the law by channelling funds to off shore accounts. Tony Blair, the former British Prime Minister lied about weapons of mass destruction to justify the invasion of Iraq in 2003.

"Who you are, what your values are, what you stand for. They are your anchor, your north star. You won't find them in a book. You'll find them in your soul." – **Anne Mulcahy**

In May 2009 the lavish expenses claimed by British MPs were highlighted in the pages of the *Daily Telegraph*. The revelations included interest on ghost mortgages, lavish refurbishments, maintenance of swimming pools and tennis courts, cleaning of moats, the purchase of manure and the avoidance of capital gains tax. Some politicians claimed that these expenses were allowed within the rules but to right-minded people the expenses seem unethical and irresponsible. Others, because of public pressure, have admitted the errors of their ways and refunded the amounts involved. Some ministers have been forced to resign because of the scandal and the position of the British Prime Minister, Gordon Brown, was undermined.

Recruitment specialists are aware that many job applicants routinely lie on their CVs. Lies range from altering lengths of time spent at individual companies to cover up periods of unemployment, exaggerating their level of experience, to understating their age. A 1999 report from the Association of Search and Selection Consultants in the UK, says that a quarter of CVs contain white lies or blatant fabrication. This highlights the need for companies to check out the claims and references of job applicants.

Cheating has contaminated all areas of sport. Steroids and other performance enhancing drugs are commonplace. Drug testing of athletes is now a matter of routine in most sports and competitions. Soccer players have been bribed to throw matches and jockeys have been bribed to throw races. Even boxers have been bribed to throw fights.

Plagiarism is a type of deceit where you steal from the writings of others and claim them as your own original work. Plagiarism is common amongst students and is facilitated by modern technology and the resources on the internet. *The Guardian* reported on 3 April 2009 that eight parents and teachers have been jailed in China after using hi-tech communication devices such as scanners and wireless earpieces to transmit exam answers, to help pupils cheat in college entrance exams. In Britain and elsewhere people have been paid to sit exams for someone else. Some experts have suggested that large universities should fingerprint students to stop friends taking exams for them. It is now feared that thousands of students use their mobile phones to send text messages to friends to get answers or to access the internet during tests.

"When you take stuff from one writer it's plagiarism; but when you take it from many writers, it's research." – **Wilson Mizner**

Unfortunately, sometimes it doesn't pay to be honest. Whistleblowers often suffer great personal hardship and unhappiness because of their principles of honesty and integrity.

For example, Dr. Andrew Millar, a director of clinical research at British Biotech, was fired after highlighting drug trials that went wrong. Millar took the firm to court for libel and wrongful dismissal and was awarded a £250,000 out-of-court settlement. In another case, Stanley Adams blew the whistle on his Swiss-based employer Hoffman La Roche in 1973 about price fixing. He paid an enormous personal price for his honesty. He was charged under Swiss law with giving away economic secrets to a foreign power and had to flee to Britain. He was eventually awarded compensation by the EC after spending years of frustration and unhappiness trying to clear his name.

HYPOCRISY

People who say one thing and do the opposite lose their credibility. Teachers who warn their pupils about the health hazards of smoking and then are seen smoking during their breaks are seen as hypocrites. An obese Minister for Health is unlikely to have much credibility when advising the rest of us to eat sensibly and exercise frequently. Authority figures should lead by example. Politicians who practise double standards and engage in concealments and obfuscations are hypocritical. The politician who teaches family values and at the same time cheats on his wife is a hypocrite. The priest who teaches that sex outside marriage is wrong while at the same time having a mistress is a hypocrite. The priest or politician who leads an anti-gay crusade but at the same time is a closet homosexual is a hypocrite. The executive who preaches probity while simultaneously fiddling corporate expenses is a hypocrite. Senior executives are hypocritical when they advocate income restraint for employees but at the same time award themselves exorbitant salary increases and bonuses. A Prime Minister is seen as hypocritical if he advises the citizens of a nation during a recession to tighten their belts while at the same time enjoying an extravagant lifestyle.

"To believe in something, and not to live it, is dishonest." – **Mahatma Gandhi**

Society condemns drug dealers and drug-related crime while at the same time the middle classes take drugs themselves keeping the drug dealers in business. Society tolerates drug taking by celebrities such as Kate Moss and Pete Doherty and even celebrates their success and confirms their lifestyles by interviewing these people on TV chat shows. Labour politicians champion equal educational opportunities while at the same time sending their own children to private schools. During the sixties, when sexual abuse was rampant in religious industrial schools, the Irish minister of culture banned the books of Edna O'Brien. He said they were a smear on Irish womanhood which encouraged a priest in her home town in County Clare to organise a public burning of the offending texts.

Despite the incontrovertible evidence that many priests break their celibacy vows, and that homosexuals and paedophiles are active within the ranks of the clergy, the pope sees no hypocrisy in making papal pronouncements to the faithful on homosexual practices, the sinfulness of sex outside marriage and the evils of contraception. It was only in the thirteenth century that St. Thomas Aquinas invented the doctrine that sex was designed by God for procreation only and that all other forms of sexual activity were sinful. This is still the position of the Catholic Church today despite the advances in psychological knowledge.

DECLINE IN ETHICAL VALUES

Margaret Thatcher in the UK and Ronald Regan in the US believed that market forces were best and promulgated and reigned over the philosophy of individualism and free enterprise in the Western world. Thatcher is reputed to have said that there was no such thing as society but that every individual should look after themselves. Consequently, individualism and selfishness has become the norm in Western society with poverty seen as self-inflicted. Regulation of business was despised and deregulation advocated so that market forces could reign supreme. Fraud, greed and corruption have thrived within the corporate sector because of the lack of official scrutiny and regulation.

> **"The ideals which have lighted me on my way and time after time given me new courage to face life cheerfully, have been Truth, Goodness, and Beauty. The ordinary objects of human endeavour ... property, outward success, luxury – have always seemed to me contemptible."** – Albert Einstein

This philosophy of selfishness has given rise to rampant greed in the developed world resulting in reckless lending, and during 2008 the collapse of the stock exchange, the banking system, the housing market and many large enterprises. It has also triggered the worst recession in living memory bringing unemployment and financial misery to many. The rot started with the demise of Enron and WorldCom with their fraudulent accounting practices and has spread throughout the developed world since then. Many of these accounting practices were unethical but legal. Large banks have collapsed and even the car industry in the US had to be bailed out by the government.

In May 2009 the Ryan Report highlighted institutional abuse in Ireland and the publicity generated in the world press has brought shame and disrepute to the country. Children were sexually, physically and emotionally abused in homes and industrial schools run by Catholic religious orders like concentration camps. Official agencies such as the Department of Education, police and health boards, as well as the general public, turned a blind eye to what was going on. The suffering and unhappiness was beyond belief and many still carry psychological and emotional scars as adults. How dedicated religious and followers of Jesus Christ behaved in such a despicable fashion towards children in their care beggars belief. It is ironic that religious who set themselves apart as the moral guardians and role models were themselves totally deficient in morality, ordinary humanity and ethical standards.

> *"Throughout the 1980s, we did hear too much about individual gain and the ethos of selfishness and greed. We did not hear enough about how to be a good member of a community, to define the common good and to repair the social contract. And we also found that while prosperity does not trickle down from the most powerful to the rest of us, all too often indifference and even intolerance do."* – Hilary Rodham Clinton

The rise of individualism has been accompanied by the decline in moral and religious values and the rise of criminality and alcohol and drug abuse. The disappearance of religious sanctions has created a moral vacuum and a dearth of deference in the Western world. In a democracy everybody is equal and so everybody should be treated the same. This philosophy undermines the respect for experience, learning and qualifications. Young people have no longer any respect for authority figures such as priests, police, judges, bankers or teachers. Unlike Asian and Third World countries there is no respect for old people or for the experience and wisdom they have accumulated over many years. The only way to deal with the future is an understanding of the past. Wisdom only accumulates with time. This has not been helped by the scandals in the legal profession, police, church and medical professions. Old certainties no longer hold.

PERSONAL VALUES

In everyday life we encounter situations requiring honesty, integrity and truthfulness. The choices we make are governed and guided by our personal values and beliefs. Obeying the law, being good citizens, fair dealing, paying taxes, doing our fair share of the work, supplying valid information and providing accurate reports are just some of the common situations we are likely to encounter. We should never compromise our personal values of honesty and integrity. People who are congruent act in harmony with their values, principles and beliefs.

They walk the talk and display by their actions the sincerity of their intentions. Unhappiness, isolation, loss of credibility, stress, anxiety, poor relationships and even incarceration are some of the consequences for dishonesty and lack of integrity in our dealings with others.

Ivan Boesky in the US declared that greed was good. He had few principles and values. He was involved in insider trading scams. He was convicted and fined $100 million and spent some time in jail – so much for his "greed is good" concept. Another person lacking in principles and values was Frank Dunlop, a former Irish Government press secretary and PR consultant. He was sentenced in May 2009 to 18 months in prison and a €30,000 fine after admitting bribing councillors for their support in planning applications. Since the enquiry started in 2000 his health has deteriorated allegedly due to the stress involved and he has become a social pariah shunned by friends and former business associates. He has lost face and social esteem, brought shame to his family and has become a very unhappy and disillusioned man. He has lost his business and the respect of his friends, colleagues and of the wider community. His fall from grace was emphasised by the fact that he arrived to the court to hear the final verdict in a top of the range Mercedes but was driven away in a prison van. The politicians who received the bribes have either denied receiving them or claim that they were legitimate political contributions. They are living up to public expectations and the stereotype that all politicians are dishonest and liars. The lying and cheating culture endemic in politics prevents them from acting otherwise. Similarly, the property developers who funded the bribes have not been brought to justice. Frank probably feels he's a scapegoat as all the other parties in the episode have so far got away scot free!

"Be valued and principle based. Know what you stand for and live by those standards." **– George Fischer**

Sometimes people are easily led and may be influenced to compromise their personal values (for example to lie in order to make a sale or to cover up a mistake). The result is that people feel unhappy and bad about themselves because their sense of values and self-esteem has been undermined. Where there is a conflict between personal and corporate values it is better to leave the company and find another corporate culture that is in harmony with your conscience, personal values, principles and beliefs. You will then be truly happy as you find pride, peace of mind and satisfaction in your job.

MUTUALITY AND THE SENSE OF FAIRNESS

The opposite of individualism is the idea that we are all in this together. In Asian and Third World cultures people place greater priority on the goals and welfare of the group – family, extended family and work group. Ideas like self-actualisation and self-reliance are foreign to their culture. People should treat each other the way they would like to be treated. People should look after those less fortunate than themselves. Behaving well and treating others with compassion, consideration and fairness makes you feel good. People with a strong moral sense are happier and do better than others socially and economically. A clear conscience makes for a contented life.

According to evolutionary psychologists, the concept of sharing and fairness was developed many thousands of years ago when we were hunter-gathers. Sharing and cooperation was often a question of survival. Even children seem to have an innate concept of fairness. They learn from an early age the benefits of sharing and caring. The social philosophy adopted by society can determine what fairness means. In a meritocracy those who work hard reap the greatest rewards whereas in an oligarchy those of higher status gain most. In a social democracy the needs of the elderly, disabled, sick, less fortunate and poor are catered for. In a charity those considered to be in greatest needs get preferential treatment. In the real world people are often exploited and taken advantage of and total fairness is seldom achieved.

The principle of impartiality or fairness is an integral part of the Christian message and of Western democracy. It teaches to love your neighbour as yourself and to treat people as you would like them to treat you. The bible teaches that it is more blessed to give than to receive. The happiest societies are democracies with a touch of socialism to look after the needs of the elderly and their less fortunate citizens through adequate social welfare systems. Whether we like it or not we are all interdependent on others. In modern society we depend on others to provide us with the goods, services and facilities for a comfortable life.

"Consider the following. We humans are social beings. We come into the world as the result of others' actions. We survive here in dependence on others. Whether we like it or not, there is hardly a moment of our lives when we do not benefit from other's activities. For this reason it is hardly surprising that most of our happiness arises in the context of our relationships with others." **– Dalai Lama**

SUMMARY

An ethical life is a happy life. Unethical acts may be punished by law or frowned on by society and may cause great personal hardship and unhappiness. Ethical people act for the benefit of others rather than their own selfish interests. Moral behaviour creates trust and attracts friendship and goodwill which are important ingredients for a happy life. Ethical people are consistent and so their words match their actions. Lying and cheating will inevitably bring unhappiness. Hypocrites are people who say one thing and do another and create unhappiness for those they come in contact with. To be happy in life people need to adhere to their personal values and beliefs and treat others the way they would like to be treated themselves.

Individualism has become the norm in the West. This philosophy of selfishness has given rise to rampant greed in the developed world resulting in reckless lending and the collapse of the banking system, the housing market and many large companies. The rise of individualism has been accompanied by the decline in moral, community and religious values.

Five Activities to Improve Your happiness

1) Each and every day act with integrity, tell the truth and always do the right thing.

2) Charity is good for you and for the recipient. So give to charity as often as you can afford to benefit from the feel good factor. After all it is more blessed to give than to receive!

3) Treat others the way you would like to be treated.

4) The next time you make a promise be sure to keep it. Your word should be your bond.

5) Practise empathy when dealing with others. Put yourself in the other person's shoes to really appreciate where they are coming from. Feel and share their pain and experience their disappointment.

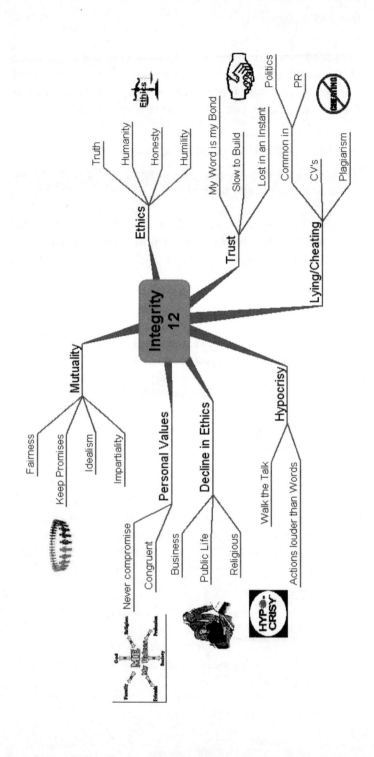

Integrity 12

Ethics
- Truth
- Humanity
- Honesty
- Humility

Trust
- My Word is my Bond
- Slow to Build
- Lost in an Instant

Lying/Cheating
- Common in
  - Politics
  - PR
- CV's
- Plagiarism

Mutuality
- Fairness
- Keep Promises
- Idealism
- Impartiality

Personal Values
- Never compromise
- Congruent

Decline in Ethics
- Business
- Public Life
- Religious

Hypocrisy
- Walk the Talk
- Actions louder than Words

13

MEANINGFUL GOALS AND PLANS

- ❖ *Why do you need goals to be happy?*
- ❖ *Why set goals at the appropriate level?*
- ❖ *Why use SMARTS for goals?*
- ❖ *Why are intrinsic goals so important?*
- ❖ *Why do you need a daily happiness plan?*

INTRODUCTION

Happiness means having meaningful goals and enjoying the process of achieving them. Goals help you get things done and can be intrinsic or extrinsic. Intrinsic goals are personal, authentic and truly your own. Extrinsic goals are what other people want you to do. Those who pursue intrinsic goals such as becoming the person you are capable of becoming are happier than those who pursue extrinsic goals such as wealth. Happy people use their **SMARTS** for goals. This means their goals are specific, measurable, attainable, rewarded, timely and supported. The main goal of life is to be happy and this aim should be supported by a happiness plan.

"Sustainable happiness is very much linked to the setting of goals and the overcoming of difficulty, and these goals must be meaningful to the individual." – **Dr. Raj Persaud**

ENJOY THE JOURNEY

Happiness depends on your perspective, your ability to improve situations by setting meaningful goals and taking personal responsibility for your actions. Goals will help you get things done. Goals are a means to happiness and not an end. Reaching the goal will only bring short-term happiness as it will often be experienced as an anti-climax. The happiness is in the journey striving towards goals. Enjoy the process and the thrill of achieving each step on the way. At the end of each goal you will need more goals and activities to keep you engaged and interested.

Life is all about setting new challenges as soon as existing goals are achieved. Begin with a vision or dream which will act as your source of inspiration. Without a vision plans are useless. Visions should be supported by goals and the goals in turn will be achieved through plans and action programmes. If you visualise what you will see and hear, and how you will feel when you achieve your goal, you are more likely to succeed. This is based on the Law of Attraction. Things that you fervently desire and do something to bring into your life are more likely to happen.

Andrew Willis shows how persistence, passion, dedication and hard work can solve seemingly insolvable problems. Andrew became obsessed with solving Fermat's Last Theorem, a problem that had beaten mathematicians for 350 years. In 1993, after seven years of intense work and more than 15,000 hours, he presented his proof of the theory to a conference in England. A handful of peer reviewers found several small errors and Willis set about addressing them. After a further year of work Willis satisfactorily met the criticisms of his peer reviewers and solved the theorem to everybody's satisfaction.

"I know the price of success: dedication, hard work, and an unremitting devotion to the things you want to see happen." – **Frank Lloyd Wright**

Goals Should Offer Challenge

It is important that goals are set at the appropriate level. Expectations should be realistic. Goals set too high are beyond your capabilities and will lead to frustration and disappointment. Goals set too low will offer little challenge and create boredom. You need to be stretched so that goals should be set at the appropriate level to achieve this. Such goals will motivate you by driving you forward with eagerness and anticipation. Identify likely obstacles so that you will have contingency plans to overcome them. Worthwhile goals are seldom easy to attain and this provides the challenge. Make it happen by having action plans, programmes, sub-goals and interim targets. The key is action. Good intentions are useless unless they are executed.

Goals give you a sense of purpose and control over your life. Longitudinal studies of students at college who set goals showed that they went on to lead more successful and happier lives than students who failed to set goals. People who set goals know where they are going, which bolsters their self-esteem and makes them feel more efficacious and confident. People who don't set goals just drift aimlessly through life.

"Give me a stock clerk with a goal and I'll give you a man who will make history. Give me a man with no goals and I'll give you a stock clerk." – J.C. Penney

---

Goals provide structure and meaning to daily life and will help you cope with problems. Sometimes you will need to substitute new goals for unattainable ones. You need to be flexible in our approach in line with the challenges that confront you. You need different goals for different stages and challenges of your life such as going to college, starting work, settling down, rearing children, midlife and retirement. Each of these stages provides unique challenges and opportunities to learn and exercise problem-solving skills.

TYPES OF GOALS

The types of goals can be intrinsic or extrinsic. Intrinsic goals are personal, authentic and truly your own. You have a vision of the type of person you want to be or life you want to lead. Intrinsic goals are freely chosen to give you direction, meaning and purpose to your life. They are inherently satisfying providing the primary driving force for your existence. They are meaningful because they are rooted in your interests, inclinations, core values, beliefs and aspirations and in harmony with all the areas of your life. Intrinsic goals will become a self-fulfilling prophecy and so you will be more likely to achieve them.

Extrinsic goals are what other people desire you to do. These people are operating to their own agenda and not yours. Therefore extrinsic goals are likely to be inauthentic and conflicting with your feelings and needs. Peer pressure from family, friends and managers can undermine intrinsic goals and compel you to follow goals that you don't really want to do, don't really care about or don't really enjoy pursuing. They may even offer financial and other inducements to achieve the goals. However, you are less likely to attain them because you really don't feel that they're your own.

"If you find a path with no obstacles, it probably doesn't lead anywhere." – **Frank A. Clarke**

HAPPY PEOPLE HAVE THE SMARTS FOR GOALS

SMARTS is a well-known acronym for setting and remembering the essential elements of effective goals. It stands for:

- **S**pecific. Goals should be vivid, clear, concrete and crystallised in writing. Specify the goals in a way that you find compelling. Saying to yourself to "do your best" on a task is too vague. Similarly, asking yourself to reduce your weight is not specific enough. This could mean one per cent, two per cent or any reduction. Vague goals will only produce vague results. Better to say that at the end of the week you will have lost two pounds and that at the end of a month you will have lost five pounds. Unwritten goals are like seeds without soil. Some authorities maintain that goals written down are 20 times more likely to be achieved than goals not made explicit. Use your imagination to visualise where you want to be and mentally rehearse the steps you must take to get there.

- **M**easurable. What can't be measured is rarely done. If you can't measure it, you can't manage it. Break down your main goals into sub-goals and create time targets for each. Divide and conquer should be your motto. As the saying goes, "life is hard by the yard, but by the inch it's a cinch". Chunking goals into smaller elements makes them more feasible and achievable. Remember, the way to eat an elephant is one bite at a time. Progress goals create motivation and interest and a sense of achievement on the accomplishment of each step. Have regard to quality, quantity, time and cost. These factors will act as benchmarks and help you plan and control your activities. They will also indicate when your goals have been achieved. In the meantime, corrective action may be needed to bridge the gap between the desired and actual situation and put you back on target again. The important point is that goals should be defined precisely so that progress can be measured.

- **A**ttainable. Goals should be challenging but not unreasonably difficult. If you feel a goal is unrealistic you will not be committed to it. In other words, don't set yourself up for failure by setting unrealistic goals. Be flexible. There comes a point when it makes more sense to give up and switch to a new goal, if a goal becomes impossible to achieve. In addition, those who refuse to disengage in the face of repeated failure are in danger of developing physical and mental health problems. Have confidence in your ability to solve problems and overcome obstacles on the journey to your goals. On the other hand, if your sense of self-efficacy is low you will reflect on your inadequacies and thereby undermine your ability to achieve your goals.

- **Rewarded.** When you achieve your goal it must bring some reward. Rewards should also be in place for the achievement of sub-goals so that you are motivated to keep going. This will keep you motivated and committed. The goals must be relevant and pertinent to your interests. Objectives created by you rather than by somebody else will have your sincere commitment, as they are inherently motivational. You know you have the right goals when they move, inspire and incite you to action. The right goals will be congruent with your self-image and thus in harmony with your values.

- **Timely.** Goals should be time-bound. That which can be done at any time is rarely ever done. Time constraints concentrate the mind and create a sense of urgency. Deadlines and time schedules create a challenge and focus your energies on the achievement of completion times. Review regularly to check how you are progressing. Take corrective action as necessary to keep you on target.

- **Supported.** Specify the resources – physical, financial and mental – needed to achieve your goals. Decide who, how, when and where you will need support to help you achieve your objectives. It is a good idea to let your family, friends and colleagues know what you are trying to achieve and how they can be of assistance to you. It's an extra incentive when you know others are aware of what you're trying to achieve and you feel you don't want to lose face in their eyes. Seek out a coach or mentor to achieve your goals. It takes courage to seek help when you need it. Consider any additional training or expertise you will need to support your aims.

"The more intensely we feel about an idea or a goal, the more assuredly the idea, buried deep in our subconscious, will direct us along the path to its fulfilment." **– Earl Nightingale**

When considering objectives, be aware of the difference between effectiveness and efficiency. Effectiveness is doing the right things while efficiency is doing things right. You could be very efficient and be ineffective at the same time. There is no point in doing things well if they shouldn't be done at all! In a work context, many people are doing unnecessary tasks, but doing them very well. With the passing of time and changing organisational and regulatory requirements some jobs become unnecessary but the person doing the work may not realise this. On the other hand, you could be very effective and inefficient at the same time. You may be doing the right things but your methods may be cumbersome, time-consuming and wasteful in the use of resources. Ideally, therefore you should be both effective and efficient.

"First, have a definite, clear practical ideal; a goal, an objective. Second, have the necessary means to achieve your ends; wisdom, money, materials, and methods. Third, adjust all your means to that end." – **Aristotle**

THE GOAL IS TO BE HAPPY

The goal of life is to be happy and so live life to the full. Have no regrets in old age that you haven't done what you intended to do. Discover what you want in life and be grateful for what you have. Believe that you are capable of great things if you set your mind to do so. See yourself as unique and full of potential. Develop a structured approach to happiness.

Happiness doesn't just happen by chance; you've got to make it happen. Do the things that make you happy. Start the day with a happiness plan and the intention of being happy. Happiness is the purpose of life – the goal of all goals. Begin with the same ritual. Think of five things you are grateful for in your life. Look forward to the things that you want to achieve during the day. Accomplish something worthwhile every day that brings you closer to your long-term goals. Set goals for critical areas of your life such as career fulfilment, family, time management, interpersonal relationships, financial control and recreational time.

Set daily goals. Happiness is the pursuit of meaningful goals. Don't trade morals for meaningful goals. Without meaning people fill the void with hedonistic pleasures, indulgence in alcohol, drugs, sex, power, materialism, hatred, boredom or neurotic obsessions and compulsions. Choose things that are ethical and that you want to do rather than things you feel compelled to do. Do the things that you know will lead to the achievement of your goals and make you happy. This will create the right positive mental set.

It's counterproductive to have a narrow focus and a single goal. There is an abundance of research that supports this position, including the Grant study. This tracked a group of Harvard graduates for more than 50 years. Those with the most successful careers were not necessarily academically outstanding. However, since leaving college they did not allow their professional ambitions to dominate or control their lives. Instead, they allowed themselves to build strong, stable marriages and lasting friendships. They made room in their lives for exercise, relaxation, holidays and multiple interests and activities.

> **"What is not started today is never finished tomorrow." – Johann Wolfgang Von Goethe**

Time is a precious resource. It is too important to waste. Make sure you use your time effectively by adding value to your life. Purposely set out to improve your interpersonal and communications skills during the day. Talk to someone you like. Express feelings of care, consideration and compassion. Keep your promises. Trust others unless you have good reason to feel otherwise. Live within your means. Don't spend money you haven't got. Throw away those credit cards. People under financial stress are very unhappy. Plan your free time. Don't just drift along and let things to chance. Time management is just as important in your free time as in other areas of your life.

> *"The reason most people never reach their goals is that they don't define them, learn about them, or even seriously consider them as believable or achievable. Winners can tell you where they are going, what they plan to do along the way, and who will."* – Denis Waitley

THE HAPPINESS PLAN

Without plans our happiness objectives will never be achieved. Planning ensures that you put thoughts on paper and that everything is considered and nothing overlooked. Having a positive attitude to your work and free time will make your life more interesting and satisfying. Action plans detail the activities that you must do to reach your happiness goals. It includes considering alternatives so that you choose the activities that you enjoy doing best. The happiness plan involves:

- Setting happiness objectives for each area of your life including work, community involvement, family and recreational time. This will ensure that you will lead a happy, balanced life.

- Deciding what to do to become happy by setting down the detailed activities you need to undertake to be happy. Only you know and can identify what makes you happy. These might include work activities, learning and development activities, taking part in community projects, playing sports, recreational pursuits, visiting museums, going to the theatre and cinema, eating out, going for a walk, weekend breaks, hobbies, holidays and family time.

- Deciding when to do them in the form of a detailed schedule including starting time, duration and completion times. This ensures that nothing is left to chance and that you apply a systematic approach to recreational planning the same as you do to planning your time at work.

- Determining the resources, including time and money, that you will need to achieve your happiness objectives. Hobbies, holidays and recreational pursuits cost money, so you will need to budget for them.

- Deciding where to do it, what to do, and who to do it with, including identifying the people who are needed to help you achieve your happiness plans. These might include family, friends, coaches, mentors and work colleagues.

- Review your plan to ensure that you have achieved your happiness objectives.

SUMMARY

Goals are a means to happiness and not an end. Reaching the goal will only bring you short-term happiness. Enjoying the journey is the source of the greatest happiness. Goals should be set at the appropriate level – not too hard and not too easy. Goals give you a sense of purpose and control over your life. They give structure and meaning to everyday life.

The types of goals can be intrinsic or extrinsic. Intrinsic are in harmony with your values and provide the primary driving force for your existence. They become a self-fulfilling prophecy propelling you forward. Extrinsic goals are what other people want you to do.

The primary goal of life is to be happy. Happiness doesn't happen by chance but must be planned for and made happen. Happiness is the pursuit of meaningful goals in critical areas of your life such as career fulfilment, time management, interpersonal relationships, financial control and recreational pursuits.

Five Activities to Improve Your happiness

1) Set goals for critical areas of your life including work, home and play.

2) Enjoy the process of getting to your goals. Savour the journey

3) Change your goals from time to time so that they are in harmony with your stage of life and with your values.

4) Compile a daily happiness plan. This should be backed up by activities and time schedules.

5) Before you retire at night review how successful you were in achieving your daily goals. Bring forward those goals for action in the following day that you failed to achieve.

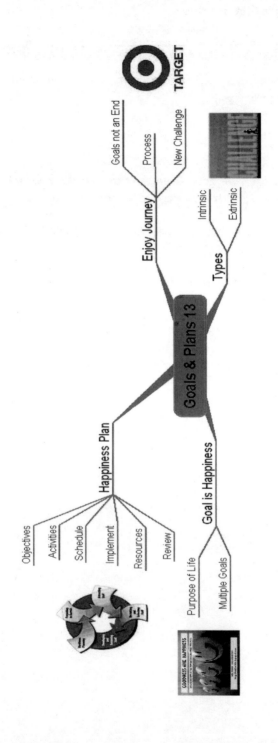

Goals & Plans 13

Enjoy Journey
- Goals not an End
- Process
- New Challenge

TARGET

CHALLENGE

Types
- Intrinsic
- Extrinsic

Happiness Plan
- Objectives
- Activities
- Schedule
- Implement
- Resources
- Review

Goal is Happiness
- Purpose of Life
- Multiple Goals

GOODNESS AND HAPPINESS

14

HAPPY PEOPLE MANAGE STRESS

❖ *How do you cope with stress?*

❖ *Who are hardy people?*

❖ *What are hassles?*

❖ *What is the hassles/uplift ratio?*

❖ *What can you do to counteract stress?*

INTRODUCTION

Managing your stress is an essential part of being happy. The Type A personality tends to be unhappy while the Type B personality tends to be happy. Hardy people take stressful situations in their stride. They draw their mental strength from the psychological approach of the three Cs: control, commitment and challenge. Problems in life can be solved if they are tackled in a systematic way with persistence and determination.

Hassles are the irritating, frustrating and niggling events that happen to you every day. Their cumulative effect can have more impact than a major stressful situation. Uplifts are little events that give you a boost during the day. If the uplifts/hassles ratio is positive it will help you cope with the little stresses of life successfully. Emotionally intelligent people have an even temperament, practise good relationship skills and thus tend to live happy lives.

COPING WITH STRESS

Hans Seyle was the first researcher to identify psychological stress. In the 1930s he adapted the idea of stress from physics and applied it to human beings. He demonstrated that the human body responds to environmental threats in specific ways. His work laid the foundation for how we understand stress and the effect it has on our mental and physical health.

A simple definition of stress is the wear and tear on the body. It is an imbalance between an individual's capabilities and the demands placed upon them. Stress is not a result of what actually occurs, but is the result of how you perceive what is happening. Stress is a mental interpretation of an external event. Short-term stress is good for you: it keeps you healthy by giving your immune systems a boost and keeps you mentally aroused and aware of what is going on around you. This makes sense in light of our evolutionary past because when we were under threat or frightened we became hyper-vigilant so that we could protect ourselves in a dangerous situation. It is chronic long-term stress that is bad as it impairs our immune system and leaves us open to illness.

Anxiety leads to stress, burnout and depression. Happy people look at the big picture and are optimistic that things will turn out well. Unhappy people are obsessed about the detail, fret over small things and think that things will turn out badly. We have the psychological resources to deal with most problems that life can throw at us. These include our intelligence, education, experience and personality.

Distract your thoughts through physical exercise or seeking out emotional support. Things are seldom as bad as they seem. Find meaning in your life by adopting new perspectives and living life to the full. An immature approach is shunning others and withdrawing into oneself. A mature approach is to analyse the problem, consult with others and reassess your priorities.

Even traumatic situations can be reframed by turning the situation into a challenge and seeing some value in your difficulty. What doesn't kill you makes you stronger. You have three options when dealing with trauma: you can survive, recover or thrive on the situation. The third option is obviously the best. People often find help in times of trouble in turning to religion or seeking out social support.

The unconditional affection you receive from your dog may have a positive effect on your health and relieve your stress. In a study presented at the 1999 annual meeting of the American Heart Association, Dr Karen Allen, a medical researcher at the State University of New York, found that stockbrokers suffering from high blood pressure showed lower blood pressure readings in stressful situations after adopting a dog or a cat than did their counterparts who had no pets. Allen doesn't know why pets lower blood pressure but surmises that "having something on your side, something you can always count on to be non-judgemental psychologically creates a beneficial atmosphere".

"The perfect no-stress environment is the grave. When we change our perception we gain control. The stress becomes a challenge, not a threat. When we commit to action, to actually doing something rather than feeling trapped by events, the stress in our life becomes manageable." **– Greg Anderson**

TYPE B = HAPPY PEOPLE

Type A and Type B personalities are based on research by Friedman and Rosenman in 1974. The Type A individual has for years been considered a walking time bomb, a heart attack waiting to happen. The Type A is seen as aggressive, ambitious and competitive. They are driven by the clock and have an ob-session with achieving more and more in less and less time. Some observers have named their behaviour "hurry sickness". Their self-esteem and sense of identity depends on their achievements. If they fail to achieve something, they become frustrated and angry. Because of their ambition, aggression and lack of patience, Type A people are not renowned for their good interpersonal skills.

On the other hand, the happier Type B is seen as easygoing and able to set time aside for fun and relaxation without feelings of guilt. Type B people are seen as having a more relaxed approach to life, where work is only seen as one of many interests. They are less likely to suffer from stress-related illness. They tend to be calm and contented, laid-back and take things in their stride. They are good at delegating, trust and cooperate with others and are well-liked because of their good interpersonal relationship skills. Type Bs are less prone to heart disease and other stress-related illnesses.

In recent times psychologists have identified an even deadlier personality than Type A. They have named it Type D, a cynical, repressed, hostile individual who finds it hard to express emotions and keeps those bad feelings bottled-up inside. Type D people are far more likely to have heart attacks and strokes and four times more likely to die of the disease. It was also found that Type D people have a diminished ability to fight infection compared with those who are more open about expressing their emotions. The finding is in line with a body of research linking social inhibition to less active immunity when confronted with infectious disease.

HARDY PEOPLE

Hardy people seem to be able to deal with disappointments and take stressful situations in their stride. Less hardy souls crumble under the stress and seem helpless. Hardy people are more likely to adopt a systematic problem solving approach to stressful issues and to solicit support when needed. They confront issues rather than to disengage, feel helpless or become highly emotional. They are less likely to waste time wishing things were better and instead do something about it. They accept that bad things happen to good people.

The hardy personality is resilient and able to bounce back after suffering significant setbacks. They are able to persevere through difficult times and return to a healthy state of being. Resilient people externalise blame and internalise success. They know that they are not in control of external events and thus may be vulnerable to danger. Even in the Nazi concentration camps, it was the hardy individuals who were able to find meaning in the horrifying situation they found themselves in and survive. Their mental strength was used to overcome their physical vulnerabilities and limitations.

> *"The components of anxiety, stress, fear, and anger do not exist independently of you in the world. They simply do not exist in the physical world, even though we talk about them as if they do."* **– Wayne Dyer**

Control, Commitment and Challenge

Hardy people draw their mental strength by adopting the psychological approach of the three Cs: control, commitment and challenge.

- **Control**. They believe if they are going to pull through it's up to them. Hardy people believe that they are in control of and can influence situations. They believe they have the internal resources to deal effectively with the situation in the form of their intelligence, creativity, courage and perseverance. On the other hand, non-hardy people believe that their lives are controlled by other people, fate or chance.

- **Commitment**. Hardy people believe in getting involved in solving their own problems. They are players rather than spectators. They have a sense of purpose and feel passionate about what they want to do. In every area of their lives they are committed. They are committed to their family, friends and community and allocate sufficient time to nurture these areas of their life. They are committed to their career and want to do the best they can and pursue lifelong learning to prepare them for future opportunities. They are committed to their hobbies and recreation and want to be as happy as they can be. They know that an appropriate work–life balance is essential for psychological well-being. They are committed to politics and support the party they think will do the best job for their country. They show this commitment by voting in general elections.

- **Challenge**. They see problems as challenges instead of catastrophes or crises. They are aware that in Chinese the word conflict means both danger and opportunity. Setbacks during their lives like redundancy are seen as opportunities to turn a lifelong hobby into a profitable occupation. They see that a bad situation can often be turned into something better. They believe that unfortunate situations often have the potential for a happy ending. They are continually looking for challenges and opportunities. Setting challenges for ourselves and meeting them is one of the greatest routes to happiness and will energise you for further challenges.

"In times of great stress or adversity, it's always best to keep busy and to plough your anger and energy into something positive." – Lee Iacocca

---

HOW TO TURN A POTENTIAL DISASTER INTO AN OPPORTUNITY

Problems in life can be solved if they are tackled in a systematic way with persistence and determination. The following approach is suggested:

- Define the stressful situation. Symptoms may help you identify the problem but they should not be confused with real causes. Apply the questioning approach of What? Why? When? How? Where? and Who?

- Reframe the problem as an opportunity. Turn the problem on its head.

- Identify the resources that can be used to transform the situation. These will include your own psychological resources and the support of others.

- Develop an action plan.

- Implement the plan. Choose to work at managing the situation rather than drifting along waiting for others to take action. Revive the plan as needed to get the job done.

- Celebrate that you turned what looked like a potential crisis into a success.

HASSLES VS UPLIFTS

Hassles are the irritating, frustrating and niggling events that happen to you every day. They include a poor night's sleep, losing one's car keys, computer crashes, tight deadlines, late running flights, trains or buses, waiting in queues, dealing with an automated telephone system, inability to start your car, traffic jams, long commutes to work, catching the common cold and poor service in a restaurant. Small hassles can eventually take their toll. Little stresses and seemingly unimportant things can keep you from feeling happy. Cumulatively, they can wear you down. In fact, their cumulative effect can have more impact than a major stressful situation.

"To be free of destructive stress don't sweat the small stuff and by realising that all stuff is small." – **Author Unknown**

People in lower socioeconomic groups are exposed to more hassles, simply because they have less financial, emotional, educational and material resources to deal with the daily events of life. They might find it very difficult to deal with authority figures and assert their right to entitlements. In particular, minority groups often suffer discrimination during their daily lives. They may also have language problems and be constantly misunderstood which is a considerable source of frustration.

Uplifts are little events that give you a mental boost during the day. They don't make you happier but they do buffer you from unhappiness. They include unexpected compliments, finishing an important task, a friend treating you to lunch, socialising with friends and family and so on. If the uplifts/hassles ratio is positive it will help you cope successfully. On the other hand, if the uplifts/hassles ratio is negative you could be feeling the pressure and beginning to feel stressed.

ADOPTING THE RIGHT MENTAL APPROACH

Emotionally intelligent (EI) people have acquired the right mental discipline, even temperament and good relationship skills to live a happy and successful life. EI people know how to keep their anger in check, control their annoyance, withstand pressure and regulate stress. EI people are self-aware and able to read their own emotions. Knowing yourself puts you in a better position to understand and empathise with others.

Know your strengths and limitations and feel confident about your self-worth. Know how to build sound relationships by communicating clearly and convincingly, disarm conflicts with humour and kindness and build strong personal bonds. High EI is a good predictor of happiness and success in life.

"A poor life this is, if so full of care, we have no time to stand and stare." – **William Henry Davies**

To adopt the right mental approach turn negative into positive thoughts. Turn tension into relaxation and agitation into calm. Turn anger into love and sadness into joy. Turn alienation into connection, irritation into patience and chaos into harmony. Lift your spirits by:

- Treating yourself to something unusual

- Meditating

- Thinking about past positive experiences

- Enjoying a glass of wine

- Visiting a nice restaurant with your partner

- Reading an inspiring book

- Listening to your favourite music
- Taking a short holiday break in a hotel
- Going abroad to your favourite destination.

DEPRESSION

The Diagnostic and Statistical Manual of Mental Disorders defines depression as five or more of a constellation of nine symptoms. These range from depressed mood and suicidal thought to fatigue, insomnia and difficulty concentrating that last for more than two weeks. The symptoms must be severe enough to interfere with the person's social life and normal activities. Depression should not be confused with normal sadness. Physical symptoms can be acute and distressing but these should diminish with the passage of time. Jilted lovers and people who have lost their jobs or failed to get a desired promotion are entitled to feel sad. Crying is a natural human reaction to such situations and is good because it releases psychological tensions and repressions.

"Depression is the inability to construct a future." – **Rollo May**

The Law of Sadness argues that Darwinian natural selection has equipped us to be sad and this is quite normal. We are built to be saddened by loss, just as we are built to be energised by success. Even quite profound sadness lasting over a month which, say, was triggered by a failed romance, can be perfectly consistent with the proper functioning of our mental sadness mechanism. After all, sadness or melancholy was the inspiration behind much art, poetry, literature, songs and music. In fact, it is difficult to know what happiness is unless you have experienced sadness. However, in most cases of sadness, feelings of anguish will dissipate over time with the support of your family and friends. Psychiatrists believe that jotting down bad feelings, memories, or stressful thoughts on paper can help you get out of depression faster. It is only when sadness lingers on for an excessively long time and evolves into depression that professional medical advice should be sought.

Extreme stress experienced over a long time can lead to depression and burnout. Burnout is a state of physical, emotional and mental exhaustion caused by prolonged involvement in work that is too intellectually and emotionally demanding. It is mostly associated with the so-called caring professions who, on a day-to-day basis, interact extensively with others often in unhappy, emotional or tragic circumstances. These include doctors, psychiatrists, nurses, teachers, police officers and social welfare officers. In addition to its personal consequences, burnout may result in substantial costs for an organisation due to high staff turnover, absenteeism and reduced productivity.

Women are more prone to anxiety and depression than men. In national surveys of global happiness, women consistently report much higher levels of depression – twice the rate of men. They tend to seek counselling more frequently and take medication for anxiety more often than men. In Western cultures, women generally have more intense emotions, both pleasant and unpleasant, than do men. Women's more traditional roles as caretakers within the family may subject them to greater stress. The burden of caring for sick and old parents also may fall on the women in the family.

"You largely constructed your depression. It wasn't given to you. Therefore you can deconstruct it."
– Albert Ellis

Depression and High Achievers

Many famous people suffered from depression and yet went on to live successful and productive lives. They seemed to be driven by their illness to greatness. Sigmund Freud (1856-1939), known as the Father of Psychoanalysis, suffered bouts of depression and despair. He forever changed the world's view of the human mind with radical concepts such as the Oedipus complex, free association, dream theory, and the division of the mind into the id, ego and superego.

Isaac Newton (1652-1727) suffered from mild schizophrenia and manic depression. His illness seems to have inspired his discovery of calculus, the laws of mechanics and gravity. In one manic period during his early 20s, during which he made most of his discoveries, Newton worked night and day – often forgetting to sleep, eat and bathe.

Winston Churchill (1874-1965) suffered from depression but learnt to live with it and pursued a very successful career in the army and politics. During his lifetime Churchill made frequent references to his depression, which he called his "black dog". According to his close friend, Lord Beaverbrook, Churchill was always either "at the top of the wheel of confidence or at the bottom of an intense depression".

Vincent Van Gogh (1853-1890), the famous artist, struggled with depression during his short life of 37 years. It eventually got the better of him and he committed suicide on the 29 July 1890. Writing to his brother in 1882, not long after embarking on his career in painting he said, "What am I in the eyes of most people, a nonentity, an eccentric, or an unpleasant person – somebody who has no position in society and will never have; in short, the lowest of the low." Compare this self-evaluation with the world fame and renown he now enjoys! His mood swings helped him create a prodigious output of paintings during his lifetime.

Symptoms of Depression

If you feel you have any of the following symptoms you should seek medical help:

- Constantly feeling tired or lacking energy to do the things you want to do

- Lack of concentration

- Persistent sadness; feeling anxious or empty for most of the day

- Spontaneous crying spells
- Loss of appetite
- Feeling lonely even when in the company of others
- Thoughts of self-destruction or harm
- Sleeplessness
- Increased irritability
- Disinterest in sex
- Feelings of worthlessness
- Lack of pleasure in all, or most, activities; finding less enjoyment in activities you used to enjoy.

"One of the symptoms of an approaching nervous breakdown is the belief that one's work is terribly important." – Bertrand Russell

SUMMARY

We have the psychological resources to deal with stress successfully if we know how to access and use them. Distract your thoughts by using physical exercise or seeking out emotional support. Things are seldom as bad as they seem. The Type B personality type is more likely to be happy. Hardy people are more likely to adopt a systematic problem solving approach to solving stressful situations. They are resilient and able to bounce back after suffering significant setbacks. They derive mental strength by applying the three Cs to stressful situations. These are control, commitment and challenge.

Hassles are the annoying and irritating events that happen to you every day. Small stresses can eventually wear you down and take their toll. Their cumulative effect can have more impact than a major stressful situation. Uplifts are little events that give you a mental boost during the day. If the uplifts/hassles ratio is positive it will help you successfully cope with the little stresses of life. You can counteract stress and lift your spirits by treating yourself, meditating, by thinking about past positive experiences and by reading an inspiring book. People suffering from depression are very unhappy.

Five Activities to Improve Your happiness

1) Don't sweat the small stuff. Put things in perspective.

2) Learn the three mental approaches that hardy people use to tackle stress: control, commitment and challenge

3) Learn the stress busting systematic problem solving approach. Apply it in your daily life.

4) Take time out to lift your spirits when you are feeling down. Treat yourself, visit a nice restaurant or take a short holiday break.

5) Seek medical advice if you have some or many of the symptoms of depression.

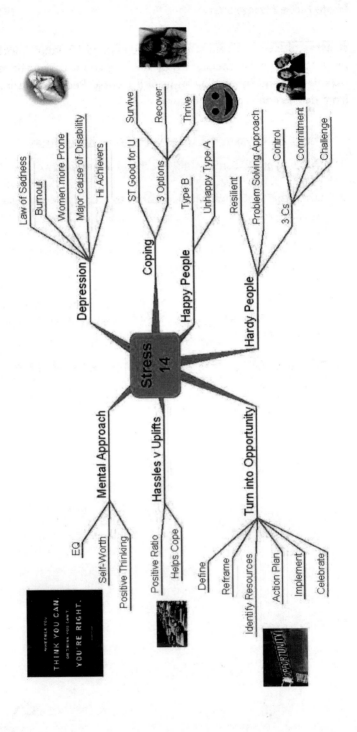

Stress
14

Depression
- Law of Sadness
- Burnout
- Women more Prone
- Major cause of Disability
- Hi Achievers

Coping
- ST Good for U
- 3 Options
  - Survive
  - Recover
  - Thrive

Happy People
- Type B
- Unhappy Type A

Hardy People
- Resilient
- Problem Solving Approach
- 3 Cs
  - Control
  - Commitment
  - Challenge

Mental Approach
- EQ
- Self-Worth
- Positive Thinking

Hassles v Uplifts
- Positive Ratio
- Helps Cope

Turn into Opportunity
- Define
- Reframe
- Identify Resources
- Action Plan
- Implement
- Celebrate

WHETHER YOU
THINK YOU CAN,
OR THINK YOU CAN'T
YOU'RE RIGHT.

15

POSITIVE AND NEGATIVE EMOTIONS

❖ *What are the positive emotions for happiness?*

❖ *Why should you practise gratitude, compassion, forgiveness and humility?*

❖ *What are the negative emotions causing unhappiness?*

❖ *What are the antidotes to negative emotions?*

INTRODUCTION

The positive emotions for happiness include courage, gratitude, compassion, forgiveness, humility, generosity and hope. Courage is about having the mettle to speak out about something you feel is wrong. Gratitude is about appreciating the things that you have. Compassion is a great awareness and sympathy for the suffering of others.

Forgiveness is the act of pardoning someone for a mistake or wrongdoing and creates a sense of inner peace and happiness. Humility is the quality of being modest and respectful. Generosity is kindness and the capacity to give money, help or time freely. Hope is a wish for something positive to happen in the future.

Anger is a feeling of extreme annoyance and is one of the biggest blocks to happiness. To maintain a happy outlook it is essential to control our negative emotions.

COURAGE

We associate courage with physical acts of bravery like going to the rescue of a colleague under enemy fire in a war situation. However, ordinary day to day happenings demand their own sort of courage. These might include standing up to a manager who is a bully, taking responsibility for a mistake or speaking out against something that you feel is unjust. Courage is motivated not by fearlessness, but by a strong sense of duty. People with principles and values are compelled to take action when they see something they consider wrong irrespective of the consequences. Living in accordance with your conscience boosts your self-esteem and makes you happier and more contented.

> *"Courage, it would seem, is nothing less than the power to overcome danger, misfortune, fear, injustice, while continuing to affirm inwardly that life with all its sorrows is good; that everything is meaningful even if in a sense beyond our understanding; and that there is always tomorrow."*
> **– Dorothy Thomson**

GRATITUDE

Modern consumerism persuades us to fixate on what we don't have, rather than on what we already enjoy. Bertrand

Russell, the English philosopher, said, "to be without some of the things you want is an indispensable part of happiness". Gratitude is about appreciating the things that you have that bring happiness into your life. Be grateful for your family, your friends, your home and all the other things that you have. Be grateful for the things you take for granted, such as running water and electricity. Many people around the world haven't these simple amenities. Gratitude is about counting your blessings.

"I cried because I had no shoes, until I met a man who had no feet."- Persian saying

---

You always have something in life to be grateful for. Be grateful for your health which most people just take for granted until they get sick and then appreciate what they've lost. Each morning you should be grateful for waking up alive with the prospect of a wonderful day in store. Be grateful for the sunset in the evening. Be grateful for the love and generosity of your partner, family and friends. Thank God for your talents and the energy and determination he has given you to use them.

"Gratitude is the key to a happy life that we hold in our hands, because if we are not grateful, then no matter how much we have we will not be happy – because we will always want to have something else or something more." - **Brother David Steindl-Rast**

COMPASSION

Compassion is having an awareness and sympathy for the suffering of others. People with compassion have a sense of commitment, responsibility, respect and empathy for the pain of others and wish to do something to alleviate the suffering of others.

The hospice movement throughout the world which offers respite and palliative care for the dying are motivated by compassion and concern for the welfare of others at a time when people are at their most vulnerable and need comfort the most as they face death.

> **"If you want others to be happy, practise compassion. If you want to be happy, practise compassion." – Dala Lama**

People with compassion are not self-absorbed, and have non-violent, non-harming and non-aggressive personalities. They have a deep sensitivity for the feelings of others. If people treat you with compassion it makes you happy. If you treat others with compassion it makes them happy. The more warmth you give, the more you will receive in return. Therefore compassionate people enjoy physical and emotional health benefits from the exercise of compassion. On the other hand, those without compassion, like the tyrants Hitler, Stalin and Idi Amin, are capable of gross acts of human cruelty and destruction and acting without pity or remorse. They often have lonely or violent deaths.

FORGIVENESS

Forgiveness is the act of pardoning someone for a mistake or wrongdoing. To forgive others you must first forgive yourself for your past misdeeds and your present faults. This gives you the opportunity to get on with your life instead of berating yourself over and over again for past mistakes. The act of forgiveness creates a sense of inner peace and happiness. It breaks the cycle of hatred and prevents the perpetuation of grudges, hostility and revenge. Holding grudges and resentments is bad for your health and those who hold them are more prone to heart attacks. Grudges can become obsessive and poison your mind. Not forgiving creates a self-fulfilling prophecy where you continually search for more evidence why the person cannot be trusted. It makes you a prisoner of the past. Forgiveness is good for both your physical and mental health. So what's the point in holding a grudge?

> *"To forgive is the highest, most beautiful form of love. In return, you receive untold peace and happiness."* **– Robert Muller**

Nelson Mendela is probably the paragon of forgiveness in the modern world. After spending 26 years in jail for his part in resisting apartheid in South Africa, he has never shown hatred, self-pity or advocated revenge for those who stole his freedom for so many years. Instead he has shown tremendous courage and forgiveness In the face of adversity. Forgiving is a strong element in the Christian tradition. Jesus forgave his persecutors while he was dying on the cross.

People forgive those who tell the truth and act responsibly to make amends even if they have made serious mistakes. In 1982 seven people died after being poisoned by Tylenol. Some capsules had been interfered with and laced with cyanide. Johnson & Johnson, the makers of Tylenol, are known for their caring and compassionate culture. They lived up to this reputation and responded immediately by recalling every single bottle of Tylenol from the shelves, while simultaneously developing new tamper-proof packaging. The company was not prepared to put the public's health and safety at risk despite the potential adverse effects on profits. As a result they retained their customer loyalty and confidence and increased market share.

> *"We must develop and maintain the capacity to forgive. He who is devoid of the power to forgive is devoid of the power to love. There is some good in the worst of us and some evil in the best of us. When we discover this, we are less prone to hate our enemies."*– **Dr. Martin Luther King, Jr.**

HUMILITY

Humility is the opposite of arrogance, self-importance, affectation and pride. It is the quality of being modest about your own achievements and respectful towards others. Humble people are not concerned with their own image or how they are perceived by others and are very slow to take offence. Humble people are not self-conscious and do not consider themselves to be the centre of the universe. They tend to focus on other's well being rather than their own. Like sages, they accept that they know very little and realise how much more there is to learn.

Some of the top leaders of all time include those with great humility, like the Dalai Lama, Nelson Mandela and Mahatma Gandhi. The Dalai Lama, the exiled spiritual leader of Tibet, shows no traces of arrogance or ostentation when appearing in public or when giving private audiences. Despite worldwide acclaim he maintains a genuine humility and treats all with equal respect. People with humility are more likely to forgive and they take praise and criticism lightly.

Humility is considered an important characteristic of good leaders. The Taoist, Lao Tsu, wrote:

"The sage knows himself but makes no show;
Has self-respect but is not arrogant.
He lets go of that and chooses this.
Working, yet not taking credit.
Leading yet not dominating.
This is the Primal Virtue.
If the sage would guide the people,
He must serve with humility."

"Humility does not mean thinking less of yourself than of other people, nor does it mean having a low opinion of your own gifts. It means freedom from thinking about yourself at all." – **William Temple**

GENEROSITY

Generosity is the capacity to give money, help or time freely. Giving confers as much satisfaction and happiness as receiving. As the bible says, "It is more blessed to give than to receive". Scientists who scanned people's brains as they donated to a favourite charity found that giving money lights up the brain's reward system in the same way that receiving money does. People feel happy when they give and happy people are more inclined to be generous. Even those who witness people helping and being generous to others benefit because it motivates them to perform their own good deeds. They experience an emotion called "elevation". Elevation makes people more open and loving towards others and makes them feel better about humanity.

True generosity is giving without strings attached and expecting nothing in return. There is a positive motive behind true generosity with people giving because they want to rather than feeling obliged to. For example, peer pressure may make people feel obliged to give to a particular charity because all their friends are doing so. The opposite of generosity is avarice or an insatiable desire for possessions.

Donating a kidney to a complete stranger is a unique act of altruism. Even more altruistic are people who lay down their lives for others. Altruistic people are generally happy people, as giving confers on them a strong sense that they are doing something worthwhile. The importance of altruism is taught by the major religious faiths such as Judaism, Christianity, Islam, Buddhism, and others. Altruism was central to the teachings of Jesus as highlighted in the Sermon on the Mount. It is true generosity as it is motivated to help others by doing good deeds without recognition, reward or self-aggrandisement.

> **"When you give alms, sound no trumpet before you, as the hypocrites do in the synagogues and in the streets, that they may be praised by men."**
> **– Jesus Christ in the Sermon on the Mount.**

HOPE

People are the only animals on earth that are truly future-oriented. We think about the future in a way that no other animals do. Squirrels think about the future by storing food for the winter, but that's instinct-driven. Hope is a wish for something positive to happen, especially if it seems possible or likely. Remember the old adage, "hope sees the invisible, feels the intangible and achieves the impossible". Hope can provide the energy, motivation and determination to seek improvement to an unsatisfactory situation by formulating action plans to achieve your goals.

Hope is a vital psychological resource in our lives; without it there would be little to sustain us. A common scenario for hope is a disabling or life threatening illness in oneself or a loved one. We may hope for a favourable outcome, for example, that the illness can be successfully treated, or death or disability significantly delayed. It is the hope of a successful outcome that helps us cope and keeps us going from one day to the next.

> *"The grand essentials of happiness are: something to do, something to love, and something to hope for."*– **Allan K. Chalmers**

As we grow old, we can profit from hope despite deteriorating physical health and the quality of our lives. We must try to compensate as much as possible for physical and mental decline by engaging with life, adopting a positive attitude, keeping fit, lifelong learning and continue to set life goals. Having something to look forward to and goals to achieve will give us hope. When all hope fails, there is nothing but despair and no reason to live. The more connected you are to other people, the less likely you are to succumb to despair.

ANGER

Turning to one of the negative emotions, anger is a feeling of extreme annoyance and is one of the biggest blocks to peace of mind and happiness. It is one of the most destructive emotions. Anger clouds our judgement, causes feelings of extreme discomfort, and leads to ill-feeling destroying personal relationships. It is a cause of great stress and may lead to ill health. The angriest people face twice the risk of stroke and heart disease than those with normal temperaments. People who are angry all the time are highly dysfunctional and are not pleasant people to be around. Safeguarding your heart against the effects of anger can be as simple as walking away from a row, or going for a walk around the block.

Anger constructively channelled, however, can be good. A moderate amount of anger will help you do unpleasant tasks like confronting a bully. It can also persuade others to attend to our needs when we feel we are being ignored. People are often driven by anger to put right some perceived injustice in the world. It was anger that acted as a catalyst for Nelson Mandela to tackle the injustice of apartheid in South Africa. It was anger that drove Dr. Martin Luther King Jr. to fight the injustice of segregation and discrimination in the US. It is anger that drives people to take to the streets to protest against unjust laws.

You should confront your anger, analyse the reasons for it and put it into perspective. It may not be the situation that's making you angry but the way you perceive the situation. You have a choice in the way you respond to a particular situation. Pre-empt the need and develop the inner discipline to control your anger by logically disputing the rationale behind it. Realise that you are ultimately in control of your own emotions regardless of what other people do. How you react to other people is within your control. Take responsibility for you anger. Blaming it on others is no solution.

"Holding on to anger is like grasping a hot coal with the intent of throwing it at someone else; you are the one who gets burned." – **Buddha**

ANTIDOTE TO NEGATIVE EMOTIONS

We cannot form and hold simultaneously two opposed emotions such as love and hate. Similarly, pride and humility, envy and joy, and generosity and avarice are incompatible mental states. However, they can alternate but cannot coexist. Altruistic love is a direct antidote to hatred. Neutralise anger with being composed. Neutralise envy with rejoicing at others' good fortune. Neutralise indifference with compassion. Neutralise impatience with patience.

Practise forgiveness instead of vengeance. Hate the misdeeds and not the person. Vengeance may bring a temporary satisfaction but does not bring long-term happiness. Practise generosity instead of selfishness. The seventeenth century philosopher Thomas Hobbes believed that people were fundamentally selfish. Evolutionists believe that the selfish gene ensured our survival and reproduction in the past. Modern thinkers believe that those with the selfish gene will wipe each other out and thus the selfish gene will eventually disappear from the population.

SUMMARY

The positive emotions include courage, gratitude, compassion, forgiveness and humility. Courage is about standing up for what you believe is right. Gratitude is about counting your blessings. For happiness, serenity and peace in your life, you should reflect on the things to be grateful for. Compassion is empathy for the suffering of others and a desire to alleviate it. If people treat you with compassion it makes you feel happy. If you treat others with compassion it makes them happy. The act of forgiveness creates a sense of inner peace and happiness. It breaks the cycle of hatred and prevents the perpetuation of grudges.

Humble people are not concerned about their own image. They are slow to take offence. Humility is the opposite of narcissism, arrogance and affectation. True generosity is giving without strings attached and expecting nothing in return.

A prime negative emotion is anger. Anger clouds judgement, causes feelings of extreme discomfort, and leads to ill-feeling destroying personal relationships. You can neutralise anger with patience.

Five Activities to Improve Your happiness

1) Start the morning by listing five things to be grateful for in your life. Similarly finish your day by listing five things you are grateful for.

2) Show your compassion for the disadvantaged by contributing to an appropriate charity.

3) Compose a letter of forgiveness to someone considered to have done you an injustice, but don't send it. The process of doing so will do you good.

4) In future don't boast about your achievements in front of others. Instead concentrate on the achievements of others as most people love to talk about themselves.

5) Give to deserving charities not because you feel obliged to do so but because you really want to do so.

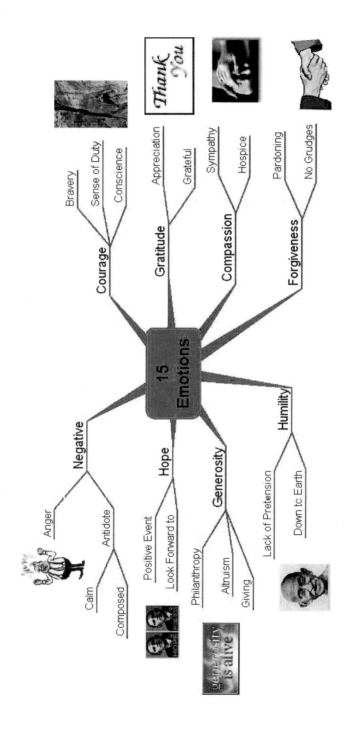

15 Emotions

Courage
- Bravery
- Sense of Duty
- Conscience

Gratitude
- Appreciation
- Grateful

Compassion
- Sympathy
- Hospice

Forgiveness
- Pardoning
- No Grudges

Negative
- Anger
- Calm
- Antidote
- Composed

Hope
- Positive Event
- Look Forward to

Generosity
- Philanthropy
- Altruism
- Giving

Humility
- Lack of Pretension
- Down to Earth

Thank You

generosity is alive

16

HAPPY PEOPLE MANAGE THEIR TIME

❖ *What is the case for time management?*

❖ *What are the two Ps of time management?*

❖ *What is the time management control model?*

❖ *How can you make best use of your free time?*

INTRODUCTION

If you want to be happy and successful in your personal life and career, managing time effectively is essential. Time management gives you a sense of purpose and control over work and recreational activities. Active people talk about making time, using time, filling time and organising time. Idle people talk about killing time. Being busy is better than being bored. The two Ps of time mismanagement, procrastination and perfectionism, waste a lot of time and cause a lot of personal unhappiness.

Happy people organise their lives so that they spend less time working and more time at recreation. To make good use of spare time we should become participants rather than spectators. Take up a worthwhile hobby to develop and utilise your skills. Plan your free time so that it is structured, purposeful and not wasted.

THE CASE FOR MANAGING TIME

If you want to be happy and successful in your life and career managing time effectively is essential. We all have the same amount of time available to us, but it is how you value time, organise it and use it that matters. Time management involves using time to create maximum personal effectiveness and efficiency. It is about planning how best to use your time and successfully implementing that plan.

Some people seem to be more time aware than others. They tend to know what their purpose and priorities are and then set about them with determination. They have developed good powers of concentration and know how to stay focused on a task until it is completed. They know how to differentiate the important tasks from the less important and then go about doing them in an efficient manner. When at work they know when to delegate and when it is better to do the job themselves.

"I recommend that you take care of the minutes and the hours will take care of themselves." – **Lord Chesterfield**

The advantages of time management:

- It helps us set objectives and achieve our long-term and short-term goals. Objectives concentrate and focus our energies. The objectives should be in line with your roles and responsibilities in life. Objectives present challenges to overcome and therefore are motivational and drive you forward.

- It gives a sense of control over our work and recreational lives. It gives you a sense of purpose by determining priorities, adopting efficient methods and allocating time to important issues. You complete important tasks on time and avoid wasting time on unimportant issues.

- It reduces stress and helps you adopt and maintain a happy and healthy lifestyle. It creates balance in your life by finding appropriate time for personal development, family and recreational pursuits. You will thus have time to relate and listen to others.

"Having kids has been a fantastic time for me. It's meant that I'm a little more balanced. In my twenties I worked massively, hardly took a vacation at all. Now, I, with the help of my wife, I'm always making sure I've got a good balance of how I spend my time." – **Bill Gates**

- It helps you avoid procrastination by dealing with problems as they arise rather than letting them grow and fester into major issues. Lack of decisiveness makes for an unhappy existence.

- It helps you develop a proactive rather than a reactive style of managing your life. Plan for the future because that's where you're going to spend the rest of your life. By being proactive you think ahead and try to anticipate what can go wrong, set objectives, plan ahead and monitor progress. This gives you the feeling that you have choice rather than continually reacting to demands of others or situations as they arise.

- It helps you become known as someone who is well organised and gets things done on time. You will feel a sense of pride when you accomplish worthwhile tasks. People under time pressure at work are unhappy, as they become obsessed with impending deadlines and are unable to pay attention to anything else.

Procrastination

The two Ps, procrastination and perfectionism, waste a lot of time. Procrastinators are unhappy because they put off everything, at work, at home and socially causing a great deal of anxiety to themselves and others. The reasons why procrastinators can't knuckle down to get a job done include the following:

- *False beliefs.* Procrastinators feel they work better under pressure. They enjoy the adrenaline rush they get from doing the job at the last minute. They operate under the false assumption that working under pressure improves performance.

- *Fear of failure.* Procrastinators would rather be seen as lacking in effort rather than lacking in ability. They fear that they lack the appropriate talent and skills to do the job and so they keep on putting it off. They do everything they can to avoid looking stupid and to preserve their sense of self-worth.

"If you want to make an easy job seem mighty hard, just keep putting off doing it." – **Olin Miller**

- *Self-control*. People who lack self-control may find it difficult to plan and prioritise. They lack the self-discipline to avoid unimportant issues and concentrate on the important ones.

- *Parental influence*. People who had very strict parents when they were growing up are prone to procrastinate. When they were children they were frequently criticised and thus are reluctant to make decisions because they lack confidence and might suffer the same fate.

- *Anxiety*. Some people procrastinate because they associate anxiety with certain tasks. For example, most of us postpone visits to the dentist.

- *Low tolerance of frustration*. You continually postpone doing things you perceive as being unpleasant like making your annual tax return. Instead you dodge the issue by getting involved in some pleasurable diversion.

"Nothing is so fatiguing as the eternal hanging on of an uncompleted task." – William James

---

Procrastinators tend to underestimate how long it takes to complete tasks. Allow yourself extra time to complete tasks in line with Hofstadter's Law, which states that every task takes longer to complete than estimated.

Apparently one sport where procrastinating might be beneficial is soccer goalkeeping. In 2008 scientists from Ben-Gurion University analysed the reactions of a number of Israeli goalkeepers after facing penalty kicks. According to their calculations, staying in the centre of the goal is the most successful strategy for stopping the ball. It works 33.3 per cent of the time as against 14.2 per cent of the time when diving to the left and 12.6 per cent of the time when going to the right. However, when the researchers asked the goalkeepers after failing to stop a penalty kick, the ones who stayed in the middle were the unhappiest because they felt they were doing nothing. Those who took some action felt better about themselves even though statistically speaking they took the inappropriate action.

Perfectionism

Perfectionism is the obsessive need to do things right and the rigorous rejection of anything less than perfect. The price of perfectionism is prohibitive and in most areas of life it is unnecessary. While it is nice to write letters of a good standard it is hardly necessary to go to adopt elaborate rituals of checking and rechecking to achieve this. Perfectionism prevents people from engaging in challenging experiences. If you're always focused on getting things right you're missing out on the opportunity to be creative and learn from your mistakes.

Perfectionists interpret mistakes as failure and they believe that making errors will lose them the respect of others. The desire to avoid mistakes means they miss out on opportunities to experiment and learn new things. For example, people learn to write by showing their work to others and getting critical but constructive feedback. Perfectionists avoid having their writing evaluated and thus miss out on opportunities to improve their writing. Success is more about learning from your mistakes than getting everything right. Look on mistakes as feedback to try something else and learn something new.

> *"Perfectionism is a dangerous state of mind in an imperfect world."* – **Robert Hillyer**

Psychologists believe that perfectionists are made and not born. They are often the children of very demanding parents who imbued them to be the best at everything they do. They are thus programmed from an early age for perfectionism.

GETTING CONTROL OF TIME

The time management control model is a useful technique. This helps you prioritise time according to importance and urgency. Importance is shown on the vertical axis and answers the question: "How does this task help me achieve my overall purpose?" Urgency is shown on the horizontal axis and answers the question: "When should this task be done?"

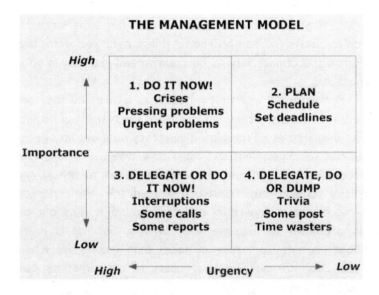

THE MANAGEMENT MODEL

	High	
	1. DO IT NOW! Crises **Pressing problems** **Urgent problems**	**2. PLAN** **Schedule** **Set deadlines**
Importance		
	3. DELEGATE OR DO IT NOW! **Interruptions** **Some calls** **Some reports**	**4. DELEGATE, DO OR DUMP** **Trivia** **Some post** **Time wasters**
	Low	

High ←———— **Urgency** ————→ *Low*

- Activities that are important and urgent should be done immediately. Crises and urgent problems must be attended to. At home a leak in the washing machine will get top priority. A fire in the chip pan will have to be put out immediately. At work a vital delivery to an important customer may get top priority. Pre-emptive action may be taken to prevent an industrial relations problem from escalating. A manager may need to take immediate disciplinary action against an employee because of a serious breach of safety standards.

- Activities of high importance but low urgency should be scheduled for a future date. In summer time getting the attic insulated may be important but is not urgent. However in winter when it gets cold the job becomes urgent in order to keep down energy costs and keep the house warm. Planning your holidays is not urgent until near the summer. As the holiday time comes near it becomes urgent and important. In work a report that has to be done in a fortnight's time is not urgent but is important. As the deadline approaches it becomes both urgent and important. Building relationships, strategic planning, preventive maintenance and budgeting will reduce the number of items in 1.

- Activities of low importance but which are urgent can be delegated or done immediately. Answering the door may be urgent but may be left to the children to look after. At work, attending routine meetings or answering routine letters or telephone calls can be given to junior staff to attend to.

- Activities of low importance and low urgency should be delegated or dumped. Junk mail can be dumped. Routine tasks around the house can easily be delegated to the children. This will free you up to concentrate on more important tasks. Generally you should stay out of boxes, 3 and 4 because urgent or not, they are not important.

PRIORITIES

Some experts categorise work into "must do", "should do" and "nice to do". Use this philosophy with advantage when planning and prioritising activities.

- The "must do" is imperative and accounts for about 75 per cent of what we do. Make sure that you don't include jobs that you like doing in your "must do" category. At home you must do your weekly shopping and you must pay bills that are due for payment especially those where non-payment may result in the disconnection of a vital service like electricity.

- The "should do" is important and accounts for about 20 per cent of what we do. Servicing the car is a "should do" job and will become a "must do" job when the service is long overdue and the car breaks down.

- Lastly, the "nice to do" are probably not central to our purpose and account for about 5 per cent of what we do. Putting up decorations at Christmas is a 'nice to do' job but is hardly essential.

"Set priorities for your goals. A major part of successful living lies in the ability to put first things first. Indeed, the reason most major goals are not achieved is that we spend our time doing second things first." – Anonymous

---

The Pareto principle is another approach to the classification of priorities. It is named after an Italian economist who discovered that 20 per cent of the population of Italy owned 80 per cent of the wealth. It is also known as the 80/20 rule – the concept of the vital few and the trivial many. This principle suggests that we waste a lot of time on trivial matters. You may discover that a small percentage of activities take up a huge percentage of time. Worst still, some of them may be of the 'nice to do' variety rather than being critical to your life. When reading realise that a small number of the words in a text convey most of the meaning. An effective reader is able to identify and focus most attention on these critical words and thus this maximises the chance of understanding the essentials of the text quickly.

MAKE GOOD USE OF FREE TIME

The purpose of many recreational activities is to make money for others rather than make us happy. To make good use of free time we should get actively involved in things. Most of us are spectators rather than participants in life. Instead of learning how to make art we view paintings. Instead of learning how to play a musical instrument we listen to compact discs. Instead of taking exercise we watch football matches. Instead of learning to cook we eat out in restaurants. Vicarious participation is no substitute for the happiness experienced in doing the real thing. So why not take up art as a hobby and get out there swimming and walking! Even Winston Churchill took up painting as a part-time hobby. Einstein played the violin in his spare time.

> *"Time is the coin you have in life. It is the only coin you have, and only you can determine how it will be spent. Be careful lest you let other people spend it for you."* – **Carl Sandburg**

We waste free time because it tends to be unstructured. It takes effort to organise free time into something meaningful that one can enjoy. Our jobs have built in goals, time schedules, feedback, rules and challenges. We should apply the same discipline to our free time. Choose hobbies that you will challenge and entertain you. They should develop an existing skill or get you to learn a new skill. This will force you to set goals and organise learning tasks.

SUMMARY

We all have the same amount of time available to us. It is how you value time, organise it, and use it that matters. Some people are more time aware than others. They tend to know what their purpose and priorities are in life and how to go about them with determination. Time management helps us reduce stress and maintain a happy and healthy lifestyle. It creates balance in your life by finding appropriate time for personal development and recreational pursuits. Time is your most precious resource. So don't procrastinate and perpetually postpone things.

The time price of perfectionism is prohibitive and more than likely unnecessary. The time management model is a useful technique for managing your time effectively. To make good use of free time we should get actively involved in events. Vicarious participation is no substitute for actual involvement. Choose a hobby that gives you satisfaction and develops your skills.

To conclude, time management is about scheduling, setting goals, planning, creating lists of things to do and prioritising. These are the core skills of time management that will help you become a happy efficient and effective person in your personal as well as your work life.

Five Activities to Improve Your happiness

1) Record how you spend your time over a representative week using a diary or time log. At the end of the week do an analysis of how you actually spend your time. Eliminate those activities that are not adding to your level of happiness and that you consider unnecessary.

2) At the start of each day draw up a 'to do' list. Prioritise the list on a 'must do', 'should do' and 'nice to do' basis. Strike off the items as you attend to them during the day. Completed jobs will give you a sense of accomplishment and satisfaction.

3) Review your list at the end of the day. Bring forward any 'must do', and 'should do' items. Consider delegating or eliminating the 'nice to do' items.

4) Chunk your work to reap economies of scale. Put certain times of day aside for making phone calls, attending to correspondence including email and doing filing.

5) Continuous self-improvement should be your goal in order to increase your job prospects, personal efficiency and effectiveness. Read books on decision-making, problem-solving, creativity, speed-reading, memory, writing, communication and public speaking. Keep your computer skills up to date.

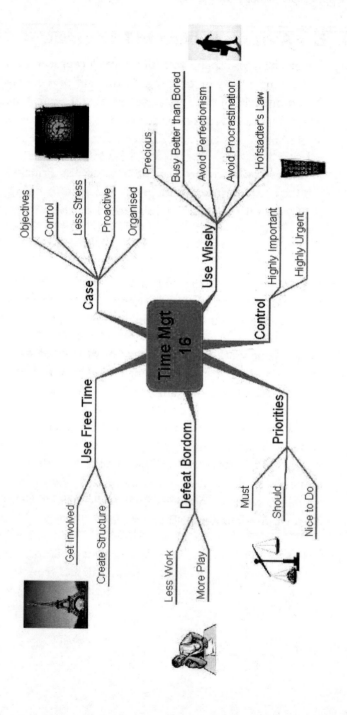

Time Mgt 16

Case
- Objectives
- Control
- Less Stress
- Proactive
- Organised

Use Wisely
- Precious
- Busy Better than Bored
- Avoid Perfectionism
- Avoid Procrastination
- Hofstadter's Law

Control
- Highly Important
- Highly Urgent

Use Free Time
- Get Involved
- Create Structure

Defeat Bordom
- Less Work
- More Play

Priorities
- Must
- Should
- Nice to Do

17

PRESCRIPTION FOR HAPPINESS

> *"Nine requisites for contented living: Health enough to make work a pleasure. Wealth enough to support your needs. Strength to battle with difficulties and overcome them. Grace enough to confess your sins and forsake them. Patience enough to toil until some good is accomplished. Charity enough to see some good in your neighbour. Love enough to move you to be useful and helpful to others. Faith enough to make real the things of God. Hope enough to remove all anxious fears concerning the future."*
> – Johann von Goethe

A prescription for happiness can be recalled by the acronym **STREETLIGHT**. This summaries the core message of this book, and stands for: Smiling and laughter, time management, relationships, emotions, effusive optimism, tackling stress, lifelong learning, integrity, goals, health and true flow. Memorising this acronym will help you recall quickly the essentials for a happy life.

SMILING AND LAUGHTER

Start your day with a smile and smile frequently during the day. It will put you in a good mood, help you feel happy and help others smile too. Smiling is infectious. Smiling helps build and support friendships. You are more likely to speak to somebody who smiles at you rather than frowns at you.

Laughter is a universal language used by people of all cultures. Laughter improves our tolerance for pain and is good for our health. Like smiling and yawning laughter is contagious. People bond through laughter and play. Laughter breaks down barriers. It is difficult to be angry at someone who makes you laugh.

One of the most sought after quality in a partner is a sense of humour. A well-timed joke can defuse an otherwise potentially explosive situation. Humour has been used in the workplace to increase productivity and create a happier workplace. Just like laughter, humour can counteract intense pain. Patients who watched comedy videos needed less pain killers than patients who watched dramas. Humour also reduces anxiety and stress.

TIME MANAGEMENT

We all have the same amount of time available to us. It is how you value time, organise it and use it that matters. Some people are more time aware than others. They tend to know what their purpose and priorities are and how to go about them with determination. Time management helps us reduce stress and maintain a happy and healthy lifestyle. It creates balance in your life by finding appropriate time for personal development and recreational pursuits. Use your down time wisely and positively for self-improvement. The time management model is a useful technique for managing your time effectively. To make good use of free time we should get actively involved in things. Vicarious participation is no substitute for actual involvement. Choose a hobby that gives you satisfaction and develops your skills.

RELATIONSHIPS

Relationships helped our ancestors survive and reproduce. Romantic relationships, family relationships and close friendships bring us the most happiness. Without sound relationships there is little scope for happiness. We are gregarious by nature. Develop the skill of unconditional love by respecting people for who they really are without continually finding fault with their shortcomings. Nurture your friendships with tender loving care if you want to keep them for a lifetime.

Accept and appreciate your partner's love. Touch is the language of love including sex, caresses and cuddles. Relationships are nurtured by love and displays of affection. Married couples are happier than single people and cohabiting couples. The sense of security and permanence that marriage offers seems to make the difference. The least happy people are those trapped in unhappy marriages. Divorced, separated and widowed people may be unhappy for many years after the event.

EMOTIONS

The positive emotions are gratitude, compassion, forgiveness and humility. Gratitude is about counting your blessings. For happiness, serenity and peace in your life, you should reflect on the things to be grateful for. Compassion is empathy for the suffering of others and a desire to alleviate it. If people treat you with compassion it makes you feel happy. If you treat others with compassion it makes them feel happy. The act of forgiveness creates a sense of inner peace and happiness. It breaks the cycle of hatred and revenge and prevents the perpetuation of grudges. Humble people are not concerned about their own image. They are slow to take offence. Humility is the opposite of narcissism, arrogance and affectation. True generosity is giving without strings attached and expecting nothing in return.

Anger clouds judgement, causes feelings of extreme discomfort, and leads to ill-feeling destroying personal relationships. You can neutralise anger with patience.

Empathy is an important part of good relationships. Empathy can be emotional or rational. To practise empathy you must understand that people see things differently. Trust is very important to friendship. When trust is broken in a marriage or friendship the relationship is permanently damaged and cannot be revived. Men and women have different communication styles. Men generally are programmed not to talk about their emotional needs while women are the opposite.

EFFUSIVE OPTIMISM

Optimism is the tendency to believe, expect or hope that things will turn out well. Optimists feel good about themselves, look at the bright side of life, see the silver lining in every cloud and focus on what's right rather than what's wrong. They are happier, healthier and more successful. Realistic optimists are prepared to move out of their comfort zone to get things done.

Optimists view problems as transient, controllable, specific and solvable. They are more resilient and bounce back quicker from setbacks. On the other hand, pessimists believe that problems will linger and that they are personal and entirely their fault. Optimists use the ABCDE approach to counteract the fallout from adverse events and reframe situations in a more positive light.

Optimism and self-esteem are not the same. Optimism is about how you view situations while self-esteem is about how you view yourself. Self-efficacy concerns our judgement about our capabilities. People with high self-efficacy believe they will succeed within their area of expertise.

TACKLING STRESS

We have the psychological resources to deal with stress successfully if we know how to access and use them. Distract your thoughts by using physical exercise or seeking out emotional support. Hardy people are more likely to adopt a systematic problem solving approach to solve stressful situations. They are resilient and able to bounce back after suffering significant setbacks. They derive mental strength by applying the three C's to stressful situations: control, commitment and challenge.

Hassles are the annoying and irritating events that happen to you every day. Their cumulative effect can have more impact than a major stressful situation. Uplifts are little events that give you a mental boost during the day. If the uplifts/hassles ratio is positive it will help you successfully cope with the little stresses of life. Counteract stress and lift your spirits by treating yourself, meditating, by thinking about past positive experiences and by reading an inspiring book.

LIFELONG LEARNING

The love of learning will help you be happier and more successful in life. Lifelong learners are naturally curious and want to know how things work. They have better paid jobs and enjoy a good standard of living. They are more likely to make sensible decisions in life and marry a suitable partner.

Education raises the level of happiness by increasing opportunities for lucrative employment and for more interesting work. Better educated people live longer because they make more informed decisions about their health and life-styles. The benefits of education include social and emo-tional competence and a sense of control. Educated people have more resources to bounce back after suffering set-backs. Education increases self-esteem by increasing your sense of self-worth. The primary purpose of play should be to raise a happy child. The benefits of play include social de-velopment and developing a sense of fair play.

Accelerated learning is fine for adults but may not be suitable for some young children. A variation of accelerated learning called hothousing has been used to accelerate the education of very bright children with mixed results. It seems to be a question of balance. Too many extra curricu-lar activities may only create too much parental pressure, anxiety, stress and even burnout in a child.

INTEGRITY

An ethical life is a happy life. Unethical acts may be punished by law and even get jail sentences. Ethical people act for the benefit of others rather than their own selfish interests. Moral behaviour creates trust and attracts friendship and goodwill which are important ingredients for a happy life. Ethical peo-ple are consistent and so their words match their actions.

Individualism has become the norm in the West. Individ-ual aggrandisement is celebrated and sharp business practice and cunning is considered a virtue rather than a vice if it brings business success. This philosophy of selfishness has given rise to rampant greed in the developed world resulting in reckless lending and the collapse of the banking system, the housing market and many large companies. The rise of indi-vidualism has been accompanied by the decline in moral, ethi-cal and religious values.

GOALS AND PLANS

Goals are a means to happiness and not an end. Reaching the goal will only bring you short-term happiness. Enjoying the journey is the source of the greatest happiness. Goals should be set at the appropriate level – not too hard and not too easy. Goals give you a sense of purpose and control over your life. They give structure and meaning to everyday life.

Goals can be intrinsic or extrinsic. Intrinsic are in harmony with your values and provide the primary driving force for your existence. They become a self-fulfilling prophecy propelling you forward. Extrinsic goals are ones that other people want you to do.

The primary goal of life is to be happy. Happiness doesn't happen by chance but must be planned for and made happen. Happiness is the pursuit of meaningful goals in critical areas of your life such as career fulfilment, time management, interpersonal relationships, financial control and recreational pursuits.

HEALTH

Your health is your wealth. Sick people would spend all the money and time they have to be healthy again. Sleep affects our mood and influences our level of happiness. A good night's sleep is important for your health and sense of well-being. The brain needs oxygen to survive. Walking provides extra oxygen to the brain and keeps the circulation system healthy. It keeps us fit, prevents us from becoming obese and gives us a sense of exhilaration and joy.

You are what you eat. Even our moods are linked to what we eat. As well as being a source of nutrients, food is a source of pleasure. Keeping to the teachings of your religion will keep you healthy and happy. All the major religions preach positive ideas like acting ethically and morally, treating people equally and with respect, practising charity and avoiding selfishness. These are all precepts for good living and a happy life. Recreation and leisure acts as an antidote to work. Leisure pursuits can be a source of joy and happiness. We need to meditate to clear our minds of mental clutter, discover ourselves and experience feelings of peace, solitude and inner calm.

TRUE FLOW

You create flow by using your skills in a challenging situation. Ordinary everyday activities like reading, writing and dancing can create flow experiences. You are more likely to have a flow experience at work than anywhere else. A well-stocked memory can be the source of mental flow experiences.

Don't postpone happiness. Happiness occurs in moments and so you should savour the moment. The senses provide great opportunities for flow. Develop your sense of sight, hearing, taste and movement. You don't have to be a professional to experience the joy and flow of dance.

There are more opportunities for flow at work than anywhere else. People find flow in work that they enjoy doing and find challenging. The reasons for dissatisfaction at work include lack of variety and challenge, conflict, boredom and burnout. There are also great opportunities for flow at play.

COLE – THE MODEL FOR HAPPY PEOPLE

- Control. Happy people are in control of their lives. Those with little or no control over their lives – such as prisoners, old people in a nursing home, disadvantaged groups and citizens of totalitarian states – suffer lower morale and poorer health.

- **O**ptimism. Happy people are usually optimistic. They expect good things to happen to them. Happiness is a self-fulfilling prophecy. The attitude you have today will largely determine how you will view the world tomorrow.

- **L**ike themselves. Happy people like themselves and like other people. They have a high sense of self-esteem and usually believe that they are more ethical, intelligent, less prejudiced and have better interpersonal skills than others. Compared with loners, those who can name several close friends are healthier and less likely to die prematurely.

- **E**xtroverted. Happy people are extroverts. Extroverts are happier than introverts whether alone or with others. They are more adventurous, have more friends and know how to enjoy life. People who care about other people are on average happier than those who are more preoccupied with themselves.

"Plant something and keep it alive. Count your blessings – think of at least five – at the end of each day. Have an hour long uninterrupted conversation with your partner each week. Telephone a friend. Give yourself a regular treat. Have a good laugh each day. Take regular exercise. Smile at strangers, or talk to them. Cut your television viewing by half. Perform an act of kindness each day."– The Happiness Manifesto, Slough social experiment, Richard Stevens, 2005

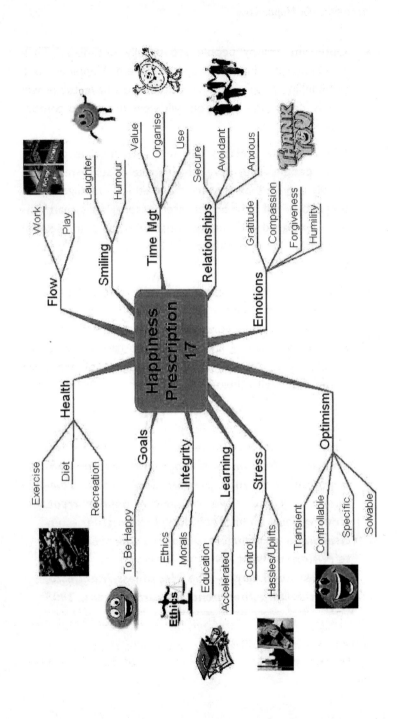

BIBLIOGRAPHY AND FURTHER READING

Amabile, Teresa M, and Kramer, Steven I. (2007) "Inner Work Life". *Harvard Business Review,* Vol. 85, Issue 5, pp. 72-83.

Barasch, Marc Ian, (2005). "Extreme Altruists". *Psychology Today,* Mar/Apr. 2005, Vol. 38, Issue 2, pp. 78-82.

Ben-Shahar, Tal (2007). *Happier.* New York: McGraw Hill.

Brooks, Arthur C. (2007). "I love my work". *The American,* September/October 2007.

Carr, Alan. (2004). *Positive Psychology: The Science of Happiness and Human Strengths.* Hove: Brunner-Routledge.

Collinson, David. (2002). "Managing Humour". *Journal of Management Studies,* May 2002, Vol. 39, Issue 3, pp. 269-288.

Coutu, Diane. (2007). "Making Relationships Work". *Harvard Business Review,* December 07, Vol. 85, Issue 12, pp. 45-50.

Csikszentmihalyi, Mihaly. (2002) *Flow: The Classic Work on How to Achieve Happiness.* London: Rider.

Culliford, Larry. (2007). *Love, Healing and Happiness: Spiritual Wisdom for Secular Times.* Winchester: O Books.

Dalai Lama. (1999). *The Art of Happiness.* London: Coronet Books.

Diener, Ed and Biswas-Diener, Robert. (2008). *Happiness: Unlocking the Mysteries of Psychological Wealth.* Oxford: Blackwell Publishing.

Dixit, Jay. (2007). "Night School". *Psychology Today*, Dec 2007, Vol. 40, Issue 6, pp. 88-94.

Doran, James. (2004). "Sex beats Mammon as the key to happiness", timesonline, 12 June 2004.

Easterlin, Richard A. (2003). "Explaining Happiness". Proceedings of The National Academy of Sciences, 23 May 2003.

Elkins, David N. (1999). "Spirituality". *Psychology Today*, Sept/Oct 1999, Vol. 32, Issue 5, p. 44.

Ellison, Katherine. (2006). "Mastering Your Own Mind Back". *Psychology Today*, Sept/Oct 2006, Vol. 39, Issue 5, pp. 70-77.

Ford, Robert C; McLaughlin, Frank S. and Newstrom, John W. (2002). Questions and Answers about Fun at Work, Human Resource Planning. Vol. 26, Issue 4, pp. 18-33.

Furnham, Adrian and Christoforou, Irene. (2007). "Personality Traits, Emotional Intelligence, and Mutliple Happiness". *North American Journal of Psychology*, Vol. 9, Issue 3, pp. 439-462.

Gentry, W. Doyle. (2008). *Happiness for Dummies*. Hoboken, NJ: Wiley Publishing.

Gilbert, Daniel. (2006). "Does Fatherhood Make You Happy?" *Time*, 19/6/2006, Vol. 167, Issue 25, p. 70.

Gottman, John. (1994). "What makes marriage work?" *Psychology Today*, Mar/Apr 94, Vol. 27, Issue 2, p. 38.

Hoggard, Liz. (2005). *How to be Happy*. London: BBC Books.

Holden, Robert. (1998). *Happiness Now! Timeless Wisdom for Feeling Good Fast*. London: Hodder Mobius.

Jenner, Paul. (2007). *Teach Yourself Happiness*. Abingdon: Hodder Headline.

Judge, Timothy A and Lleis, Remus. (2004). "Is Positiveness in Organisations Always Desirable?" *Academy of Management Executive*, Vol. 18, No. 4.

Karbo, Karen. (2006). "Friendship: The Laws of Attraction". *Psychology Today*, Nov/Dec 06, Vol. 39, Issue 6, pp. 90-95.

Lachman, Margie E. (2004). "Development in Midlife", *Annual Review of Psychology.*

Lawson, Willow. (2004). "The Glee Club". *Psychology Today,* Jan/Feb 04, Vol. 37, Issue.1 pp. 34-40.

Layard, Richard. (2005). *Happiness Lessons from a New Science.* London: Penguin Books.

Lorraine, Ali. (2008). "Having Kids Makes You Happy". *Newsweek,* 7/7/2008, Vol. 152, Issue 1/2, pp. 62-63.

Lyubomirsky, Sonja. (2007). *The How of Happiness: A Practical Guide to Getting the Life you Want.* London: Sphere.

Malone, Samuel A. (2006). *The 10 Skills of Highly Successful People,* Dublin: The Liffey Press.

Malone, Samuel A. (2004). *Surviving Stress: A Guide for Managers and Employees,* Cork: Oak Tree Press.

Malone, Samuel A. (1999). *Success Skills for Managers.* Dublin: Oak Tree Press.

Malone, Samuel A. (2003). *Learning about Learning.* London: CIPD.

Martin, Paul. (2005). *Making Happy People The Nature of Happiness and Its Origins in Childhood.* London: Forth Estate.

Matour, Susan, J.D. and Prout, Maurice F. PhD. (2007). "Psychological Implications of Retirement in the 21st Century", *Journal of Financial Service Professionals,* January 2007.

McConnell, Carmel. (2007). *The Happiness Plan: Simple Steps to a Happier Life.* Harlow: Pearson Prentice Hall.

Murphy, Annie, (2001). "Self-Help: Shattering the Myths". *Psychology Today,* Mar/Apr 2001, Vol. 34, Issue 2., p. 60.

Nettle, Daniel. (2005). *Happiness: The Science Behind Your Smile.* Oxford: Oxford University Press.

Niven, David. (2005). *The 100 Simple Secrets of Happy People: What Scientists Have Learned and How You Can Use it.* Chichester: Capstone.

Oliver, Joan Duncan. (2005). *Happiness: How to Find it and Keep it.* London: Duncan Baird Publishers Ltd.

Richard, Matthieu. (2007). *Happiness: A Guide to Developing Life's Most Important Skill.* London: Atlantic Books.

Rowan, Sophie. (2008) *Happy at Work: Ten Steps to Ultimate Job Satisfaction.* Harlow: Pearson Prentice Hall.

Ryff, Carol D. and Singer, Burton. (2000). "Interpersonal Flourishing: A Positive Health Agenda for the New Millennium". *Personality and Social Psychology Review* (Lawrence Erlbaum Associates); Vol. 4, Issue 1, pp. 30-44.

Seligman, Martin E.P. (2003). *Authentic Happiness.* London: Nicholas Brealey Publishing.

Shimoff, Marci. (2008). *Happy for No Reason: 7 Sevens to Being Happy from the Inside Out.* London: Simon and Schuster

Siebert, Al. (2006). "Develop Resiliency Skills – How valuable life lessons can breed resiliency", *T&D Magazine*, ASTD, September 2006.

Snyder, C.R. and Lopez, Shane, J. (2005). *Handbook of Positive Psychology*, Oxford: Oxford University Press.

Springen, Karen, (2004). "The Serenity Workout", *Newsweek*, 27/9/2004, Issue 13, pp. 68-71.

Stone, Michael. (2002). "Forgiveness in the workplace". *Industrial and Commercial Training*, Vol. 34, No. 7, pp. 278-286.

Vogel, Carl. (2006). "A Field Guide to Narcissism". *Psychology Today*, Jan/Feb 2006, Vol. 39, Issue 1, pp. 68-74.

INDEX